GREAT BRITISH COOKING

GREAT BRITISH COOKING

CAROLYN CALDICOTT
PHOTOGRAPHS BY CHRIS CALDICOTT

FOOD STYLING BY
CAROLYN CALDICOTT

F

FRANCES LINCOLN LIMITED
PUBLISHERS

CONTENTS

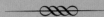

INTRODUCTION

The British Isles are fortunate. The clement, moist maritime climate has produced lush, fertile land and the perfect conditions for animal husbandry and diverse agriculture. High-quality meat and seasonal vegetables have for centuries provided the building blocks for a simple and unfussy cuisine. Slow-cooked hearty stews, one-pot broths and roast meat, backed up by dairy products, characterize the menu, with simple sauces, robust gravies and fresh herbs to accentuate flavours.

Verdant pasture has led to a plentiful supply of dairy milk, the backbone to England's cheese-making industry, with numerous regional cheeses being produced locally. A chunk of bread and a thick slice of cheese has always been the mainstay of a ploughman's lunch. Excess creamy milk is churned to make butter and buttermilk, or separated to make rich fresh cream and the extraordinary thick buttery clotted cream – essential ingredients that define English cuisine, particularly its famously indulgent puddings.

The cool waters around England's coastline provide a safe breeding ground for many varieties of saltwater fish. Traditionally these fish are simply grilled, poached with herbs and spices or baked and drizzled with brown butter or sweet spiced sauces. Cod in a beer batter, served with chunky chips, makes a favourite pub lunch, but tastes even better by the seaside eaten straight out of the paper wrapping.

Britain's native shellfish provide another treat. Oysters, once so plentiful they were considered food for the poor and were added in handfuls to pad out the meat in stews, pies and puddings, are now an expensive delicacy – more likely to be served over ice with a squeeze of lemon and a shake of spicy Tabasco and washed down by a glass of champagne, than with a pint of stout. Freshwater fish such as salmon and trout from England's abundant rivers are enjoyed delicately poached and dolloped with home-made lemony sorrel mayonnaise.

Cereal crops of wheat, barley and oats led to a healthy tradition of baking that to this day is very much alive: crusty bread, cakes, griddle scones, crunchy biscuits and flaky pastry pies. Ah, pies! Rich and savoury, sweet and fruity; raised pies, pies topped with mashed or crunchy sliced potato, puff pastry, oaty crumble – all are close to our hearts and stomachs. Barley has also provided the pie with its perfect accompaniment, real ale, starting the English love affair with the classic alehouse lunch of a pie and a pint.

The changing seasons inspired methods of preserving to provide a plentiful supply through the long winter months: cured and smoked meat and fish, pickled and preserved fruit and vegetables are still staples. And the hunter gatherer in us all will always appreciate wild game and the value of foraging, which has supplemented the pot with the flavours of wild herbs, fruit and nuts.

But one of the strongest influences on England's cuisine has come from beyond her shores: the bounty of her colourful seafaring past. Foodie treasures discovered during the long search for valuable spices, plundered from the East and the Americas has put potato into bangers and mash, curry powder into kedgeree and turkey into the Christmas dinner.

Cattle, sheep and goats were farmed to provide supplies of meat, milk and salty cheese; the first game parks were stocked with deer and pheasants; and wheat, spelt, barley and millet provided grain for bread and sweet cakes. New cooking methods, roasting and baking, largely replaced cauldron cooking. The bounty of fish and shellfish from England's rivers and coastline was an added bonus for the Romans, who were extremely fond of all things fishy, particularly, it appears, wild oysters – piles of oyster shells are a common find at Roman sites. With this new interest came the development of an active fishing industry in England.

After the fall of the Roman Empire, in the fifth century AD, Britain descended into the Dark Ages, and dark days they were for Britain's culinary history. Diet was governed by the seasons and the Church, which dictated a strict regime of fast days. The best most Britons could expect was a hand-to-mouth existence subsisting on bread, beer, porridge, root vegetables and stews made from vegetables and grain and occasionally perked up with eggs or a little meat. Most families kept a pig and chickens, and if they were really lucky they might have a cow, providing a supply of fresh milk and cheese. A lack of adequate animal feed in the winter meant that animals had to be slaughtered in the autumn. The meat was salted, dried or made into sausages, to get the people through the barren winter months. Hares, hedgehogs and squirrel became essential sources of protein and on fast days, when meat was banned, fish came into its own. Honey provided sweetness, and, when fermented with water to make alcoholic mead, a measure of light relief. Pressed apples were a welcome source of cider.

As always, the well heeled had it better. Wild game such as venison and boar was strictly the preserve of the rich, with the threat of the death sentence for poaching acting as a harsh deterrent for the hungry. For the privileged hunting was a pleasurable pastime.

After the coming of the Normans things improved again – at least for the rich. During the Middle Ages, at the tables of the wealthy, lavish joints of meat were spit roasted or flavoured with spices, citrus and dried fruit brought back to England by the Crusaders. Cheaper cuts of meat were baked encased in a simple hard pastry crust; at the end of cooking the pastry would be discarded (and left for the servants to eat). Edible flowers added scent and colour to dishes, but, oddly, fruit and vegetables were always served cooked, as it was commonly believed they carried disease when eaten raw. Table manners were yet to be refined. Communal bowls of stew and soup were eaten with a shared spoon, while trenchers – square slabs of dry bread – doubled as plates and food for the hunting dogs. Apart from the communal spoons, knives were the only other cutlery, and that was strictly bring-your-own.

The sixteenth century saw great changes at the table. The bon viveur monarch Henry VIII favoured sumptuous banquets, including vast quantities of roast meat and spiced sweet wine. Wooden trenchers replaced the rough bread forerunner. Vegetables were generally regarded as fodder for the poor, although salads of fashionable ingredients

such as artichokes and edible flowers were accepted as long as the vegetables were cooked. Soft fruits introduced from Europe also became prized garden plants; successful crops were transformed into sweet syrups and preserves.

It was inevitably a different story for the have-nots. With the manorial enclosure of common land that was once used for grazing and hay-making the less well off were left to survive on vegetable pottage, bread, cheese and whatever meat they could find: wild rabbits, pigeons, blackbirds and fish were all fair game. Foul water supplies led to a reliance on milk and weak ale to quench the thirst; wine was still the refreshment of choice of the aristocracy and drunk throughout the day.

The reign of Elizabeth I saw a period of great seafaring exploration establishing fruitful trade routes for England. Sir Francis Drake circumnavigated the world and Sir Walter Raleigh plundered the New World, bringing highly prized novelties to the table: potatoes, peanuts, pineapples, tomatoes, beans, chocolate, maize and chillies reached England's shores for the first time, and there were more exotic spices to season them: mace, nutmeg, clove, cinnamon and pepper. Rudimentary cookbooks offered practical tips on handling these exotic ingredients. Sugar became more commonly available, resulting in an eruption of desserts and puddings, including immense marzipan structures shaped into castles and animals.

In the seventeenth century, under the influence of Charles I's French wife, Henrietta Maria, sweet spiced dishes became outmoded, and were replaced at court by salty, savoury flavours. Recipe books were filled with intricate instructions on how to make delicate roux sauces and robust flavoured ragouts. Fantasy pies designed to make guests gasp exploded with live frogs and birds. And at last the English dared to eat fruit and vegetables raw, with salads becoming the height of fashion. Baking skills improved. A whole host of speciality buns, biscuits and cakes were developed, and the invention of the pudding cloth began the enduring love affair of the English with the pudding. Round plates fashioned from silver and pewter replaced the obsolete square trencher, and by the end of the century forks copied from the continent became essential tableware, with strict etiquette to match.

New methods of agriculture and animal husbandry created a proliferation in fresh produce, and markets flourished as fresh produce started to be moved more easily around the country. Turkeys from the New World replaced the peacock, and huge flocks were walked from the villages of East Anglia to the bustling markets of London. Coffee had probably first been imported into England in the sixteenth century and as it became more widely available, coffee houses became the fashionable meeting place, quickly gaining the reputation of being a hot bed of political debate and subversion. Then, during the reign of Charles II, tea, the preferred refreshment of his Portuguese queen, Catherine of Braganza, ousted coffee as the fashionable beverage of choice.

Farming innovations continued at a great pace and by the eighteenth century enough animal fodder could be grown in the summer months to feed animals all year round. Improved roads and transport enabled fresh produce such as fish from the coast to be available inland. An abundance of oysters offered the poor a cheap source of protein and oyster-sellers with baskets piled high became a common sight on the streets. Filling sustenance was offered by savoury puddings and pies, bulked out with root vegetables – including the potato, which had fallen out of fashion to become a staple of the poor.

For the rich, dinner was a lavish affair. There was still no tradition of separate courses served in succession: soup, meat, fish, side dishes and puddings were all still served at the same time. Food was extravagantly displayed on fine porcelain, the table dressed with bountiful displays of fruit and flowers. Dishes were extremely decorative, particularly the sweet jellies and blancmanges studded with dried fruit that took centre stage. Tea, still an expensive luxury, was typically served green after dinner. By the end of the century the drastic cut in the tea tax crowned tea as England's national drink. The influence of the expanding British Empire added more spicy tastes to the table. Chutneys and pickles inspired by Indian cuisine and ketchups from Malaya became essential condiments for the fashionable diner.

The Industrial Revolution of the nineteenth century also created a major revolution in how the English ate. Dinner, the main meal of the day, had always been taken around midday. With the advent of artificial light in the home, dinner, for the upper and middle classes at least, shifted to the evening. England's gentry started the day with a large leisurely breakfast. Kedgeree, creamy porridge, eggs, bacon, toast and preserves were traditionally served buffet style in generous proportions. A light informal luncheon followed in the middle of the day and afternoon tea filled the gap before dinner, which was now fashionably served as a succession of separate courses. Extensive kitchen gardens supplied wealthy households with an array of fresh fruit and vegetables. Asparagus, artichokes, kale and spinach flourished under the head gardener's care, and hot houses protected exotic fruits. England's baking became even more impressive as refined flour and imported sugar became plentiful and, most significantly, the invention of the coal-fired range enabled exceptional bakes, bread and puddings to be created. Light sponges and aerated bread now graced fashionable afternoon tea parties. Railways steamed their way across England, spreading fresh produce in their wake, although livestock were still walked to the market place.

For the workers who poured into the cities, chop houses offered good honest sustenance – beef stew, steak and oyster pudding, grilled meats and vegetables. Pie and mash shops opened their doors serving cheap and cheerful fillers such as eel pie and mashed potato. The less salubrious public houses rustled up simple pleasures to enjoy with a pint. Rarebit, a dish of wine-soaked bread topped with mustardy melted cheese, made a typical tasty pub lunch. Battered fish and chips sold from handcarts in the street became England's favourite repast on the run.

By the twentieth century intensive large-scale farming and innovations in mass food production and preservation galloped ahead at a lightning pace. Convenience became king. New farming methods and imported goods satisfied the public demand for year-round varied produce and newfangled appliances helped cook them.

But, as is the nature of the world, things have begun to turn full circle and the interest in the 'old' ways of grow your own, foraging, preserving and baking is today stronger than ever. Small-scale producers fill farmers' markets with fresh seasonal vegetables and rare-breed meat, specialist stores accommodate the proliferation of handmade cheeses, locally brewed ale and artisan-baked bread, and even supermarkets stock old-fashioned vegetables such as samphire and salsify.

MRS BEETON, THE FIRST CELEBRITY COOK

Isabella Beeton was in her very early twenties when she started working on her legendary book *Mrs Beeton's Book of Household Management*, first serialized as articles in one of her husband's publications. It was an overnight success. She pioneered the format in which recipes are written to this day, advocated the importance of local produce and revived the nation's interest in basic cooking skills – all this as well as offering practical advice on every aspect of running a household, from childcare to animal husbandry. Sadly, Mrs Beeton was only twenty-eight when she died. Her book, however, is still in print today.

THE FULL ENGLISH

We have upper-class Victorians to thank for perfecting the fine art of eating a full English breakfast. After a cup of hot chocolate served in bed, the affluent Victorian would expect nothing less than to sit down to a veritable feast of breakfast dishes, ranging from locally sourced classics to creations tinged with exoticism from the East, displayed in all their splendour on a heaving sideboard. Coddled eggs and kedgeree, cured bacon and devilled kidneys, plump sausages and juicy field mushrooms, black pudding and pie, kippers and potted shrimp, stewed figs and fresh fruit, toast and marmalade, were there to be lingered over. Even the middle classes were keen on a hearty breakfast, heeding Mrs Beeton's wise advice to start the day with a 'proper' breakfast – albeit a pared down version – to prepare for the busy day ahead. And for those on a tighter budget bubble and squeak and potato cakes became a surprisingly successful way to use up potatoes and vegetables left over from the previous day's meal.

Even with today's tight schedules a simplified Full English has endured to become a much-loved institution, and although we now probably only allow ourselves the ultimate indulgence of the 'full works' on lazy days or at the hotel buffet on holiday, the odd fry-up at the local greasy spoon never did anyone any harm. (Incidentally it also works wonders on a hangover!)

THE FRY-UP

Forget the waistline and treat yourself to 'the works': fried sausages, bacon, black pudding, eggs, mushrooms and tomatoes, with a fried slice and a mug of strong tea on the side.

This is not the time to be worrying about cholesterol, a proper fry-up is exactly what it says on the tin, everything is fried, even the bread.

SERVES 4–6
4 good quality large fat sausages
8 slices dry-cured back bacon, rind removed
4 thick slices black pudding
4 plump tomatoes, cut in half and seasoned
4 large flat mushrooms, stalk removed and cut into chunks
4 slices thin cut white bread
4–8 large free range-eggs
Sunflower oil and butter to fry

Preheat the oven to a low temperature, hot enough to heat the plates and keep the breakfast ingredients warm once they are cooked.

Add a splash of sunflower oil to a large frying pan and heat until sizzling hot. Lay the sausages in the pan and fry until really brown on all sides, half way through the cooking time add the black pudding and fry until crunchy on both sides. Place the sausages and black pudding in a heatproof dish and place in the preheated oven. Fry the back bacon in the remaining oil until the fat is golden and crunchy on both sides, add to the dish in the oven.

Add a knob of butter to the frying pan and cook the tomatoes until caramelised on both sides. Push the tomatoes to the edge of the pan, add another knob of butter and cook the mushrooms until soft, place both ingredients in the oven to keep warm.

Add a little extra oil and butter and fry the sliced bread in the juices left in the pan, until crisp and golden on both sides.

While the bread is frying, heat a splash of sunflower oil in a separate non-stick frying pan and fry the eggs (to avoid the yolks breaking, crack each egg into a teacup first before carefully tipping into the pan), as the eggs are cooking spoon hot oil over the yolks to encourage them to set on the outside and leaving the centre runny.

Place the eggs on the warmed plates and arrange a selection of the breakfast ingredients alongside and serve immediately.

FOR SOMETHING A LITTLE LIGHTER

If the Full English is just too frightening a prospect, try good old bubble and squeak or potato cakes served with a poached egg and a slice or two of grilled bacon. Both dishes are a great way to use up leftovers – or if you are really savvy you can plan ahead and cook extra in anticipation of a top-notch breakfast.

BUBBLE AND SQUEAK

The seemingly idiosyncratic name of this dish is actually purely descriptive: the potato 'bubbles' as it cooks and the spatula 'squeaks' on the bottom of the pan.

SERVES 4–6
4 tablespoons butter
1 largish onion, finely chopped
2 garlic cloves, crushed
250g/9oz shredded leftover cooked cabbage, carrots, parsnips, kale, Brussels or spinach – anything you have left over
500g/1lb 2oz leftover mash
Salt and black pepper

Heat 3 tablespoons of butter in a largish non-stick frying, when the butter starts to foam add the onion and garlic and sauté until soft.

Add the shredded greens and stir-fry until they start to brown. Add the mashed potato and seasoning to taste, and stir together until well combined.

Press the mixture with the back of a spoon into the bottom of the pan, until a cake forms. Continue to cook until brown and crunchy, shaking the pan every once in a while to make sure the bubble isn't sticking.

The easiest way to turn the bubble in one go is to place a large plate over the frying pan, flip it over and lift the pan. The bubble should be happily sitting on the plate. Add a tablespoon of butter to the pan and when it starts to foam carefully slip the bubble back into the pan. Alternatively, you can cut the cake into quarters and turn each piece individually. Continue to fry until the bubble is nice and brown.

Cut into wedges and serve topped with poached eggs.

CORNISH POTATO CAKES

These simple buttery potato cakes can be fashioned into individual cakes or one complete round scored into wedges. Serve topped with a knob of butter alongside eggs cooked in your preferred style. They can also be served spread with honey or home-made jam at teatime.

MAKES 6 CAKES OR ONE ROUND
275g/10oz leftover mashed potato
4 heaped tablespoons plain flour
60g/3oz melted butter
Salt and freshly ground black pepper
Butter to fry and serve

Mix all the ingredients together until a firm dough forms.

Turn out the dough and cut into 6 equal sized portions. Using your hands, roll each portion into a ball and then flatten into cakes roughly 1cm/½ inch thick. Alternatively, roll the dough out on a floured surface into a round, slightly thicker than the individual cakes.

Heat a large knob of butter in a non-stick frying pan and fry until golden brown on both sides. If you are making one large cake score the top into 6 wedges before turning.

Serve the hot potato cakes topped with a knob of butter.

MARMALADE

Pots of marmalade have followed the British all over the world. Famous marmalade makers Frank Cooper of Oxford still have the original tin taken by Scott's expedition to the North Pole.

MAKES ABOUT 5 X 450G/1LB JARS
700g/1½lb Seville oranges
1 large unwaxed lemon
1.35 kg/2lb granulated sugar

Wash the oranges and lemon and cut them in half. Place in a large thick-bottomed pan, and pour in 1.2 litres/2 pints cold water. Cover the pan and simmer together until the oranges feel soft when pierced with a sharp knife.

Remove the orange and lemon halves with a slotted spoon and place in a bowl until cool enough to handle. While the fruit is cooling briskly simmer the liquid left in the pan for 5 minutes.

Scoop the flesh and pith from the fruit and add to the liquid in the pan. Cut the orange skins in half and slice into thin strips. Add the strips to the pan.

Place a saucer in the freezer, ready to test the setting point of the marmalade.

Add the measured sugar to the mixture in the pan and stir over a low heat until the sugar has completely dissolved. Then increase the temperature to a brisk simmer and cook for 15 minutes or so until the marmalade has reduced and setting point is reached. To test the setting point place a teaspoon of the reduced marmalade on the prepared chilled saucer. If it sets and the skin wrinkles when pushed it is ready. If it is still a bit sloppy simmer for a little longer and test again.

When the correct consistency has been reached turn off the heat but leave the marmalade to sit for 15 minutes in the pan to allow the peel to settle.

Ladle into sterilized jars, cover with waxed jam discs and seal with a tight fitting lid. Store in a cool dark place and allow to mature for at least a month before opening.

THE BACON BUTTY

There are just three ingredients – how could anything be simpler? But there is actually a fine art to preparing a bacon butty. The bacon fat must be crisp but the meat still moist, the bread good quality and very fresh, and (in my opinion) the ketchup home-made. Add a fried egg and you have a whole breakfast in one sandwich.

Make the ketchup in advance when tomatoes are plentiful and cheap.

HOW TO MAKE THE PERFECT BUTTY

PER PERSON
3 slices dry-cured back bacon, with a good strip of fat, rind removed
2 slices medium cut good-quality white tin loaf
Homemade tomato ketchup to taste (see page 34)

Heat a griddle pan until sizzling hot, lay the bacon on top and cook for 2 minutes per side until the fat is brown and crisp and the meat a little charred.

Warm the bread briefly on the hot griddle – the bread will soak up the lovely bacon juices.

Place the bacon on top of one of the juice soaked bread slices, dollop ketchup on the remaining slice and lay over the bacon, gently pressing together as you do so. Cut the butty in half and enjoy while it's hot.

KETCHUP

The story of ketchup's origins provides a good illustration of how Britain's quest for spices influenced its cooking. Originally created in the eighteenth century, it was inspired by spicy *kechap* from Malaya, which had itself originated in China.

TOMATO KETCHUP

MAKES ABOUT 1 LITRE/1¾ PINTS
1.35 kilo/3lb chopped plum tomatoes
1 Bramley cooking apple, peeled, cored and diced
1 red onion, diced
1 garlic clove, crushed
75g/3oz brown sugar
200ml/7floz cider vinegar
½ teaspoon cayenne pepper
½ teaspoon cloves
½ teaspoon crushed black pepper
½ teaspoon ground allspice
1 cinnamon stick
Salt to taste

Place all the ingredients in a non-reactive saucepan and gently warm together over a low heat until the sugar has melted.

Increase the heat until simmering point is reached and cook for 40 minutes or so until the mixture has reduced.

Remove the cinnamon stick and blend the mixture with a hand blender or in a food processor until smooth and thick. You can either leave the ketchup with more bite or pass it through a sieve for a more traditional texture.

Spoon the ketchup into sterilized jars and store in a cool dark place.

CODDLED EGGS

Silky soft eggs lightly cooked in cream in little individual coddling pots were all the rage on the victorian breakfast table. Special coddling pots with fitted lids were designed by all the top potteries, but a small ramekin covered in kitchen foil works just as well.

CODDLED EGGS

Dip buttered toasted 'soldiers' into the runny yolk and use a teaspoon to scoop up the creamy white.

PER RAMEKIN
1 large free-range egg
1 tablespoon double cream
Freshly grated nutmeg
Salt and black pepper
Butter to grease the ramekin

To serve
Thinly sliced day-old bread
Soft butter

Grease the inside of a small ramekin with a generous amount of butter. Carefully break the egg into the ramekin and spoon in the cream. Grate nutmeg over the top, season with salt and black pepper to taste and cover the ramekin with kitchen foil.

Place the ramekin in a wide shallow pan with a fitted lid. Set the pan on a low heat and carefully pour boiling water from a kettle around the ramekin until it reaches to halfway up the pot. As soon as the pan reaches simmering point, remove it from the stove top, cover the pan with a lid, and allow to stand for 7–8 minutes.

Meanwhile, toast slices of day-old bread, spread with soft butter and cut into finger-sized soldiers.

Lift the ramekins from the water, dry on a clean tea towel and remove the kitchen foil. Serve immediately with buttered toasted soldiers.

KIPPERS

Kippers are making a comeback. A popular breakfast and supper dish in Edwardian and Victorian England, they had fallen out of fashion, but they are now firmly back on the menu. You can't beat a kipper for breakfast topped with a poached egg or for supper served with buttered slices of crusty bread.

A kipper is essentially a fat herring that has been slit down the backbone, gutted, salted, butterflied and cold-smoked over smouldering wood – an ancient process of preservation known as kippering. Watch out for imitators with added colour. The real thing should be smoked for at least twenty-four hours to achieve its golden amber colour.

Smoky, pungent kippers are wonderfully oily, so grilling and boiling are the best methods of cooking. Boiling or 'jugging' is the simpler (and less smelly) option, but grilling creates juicy flesh with a crunchy top.

Whichever way you choose to cook your kipper, it must first be prepared: remove the head with a sharp pair of kitchen scissors.

Kippers only require a short cooking time, as they have already been smoked.

To grill a kipper, line the grill pan with foil and brush both sides of the fish with a little melted butter. Place the fish flesh side down and grill for a couple of minutes, then turn the fish and grill for a further 5 minutes. Add a squeeze of fresh lemon juice before serving.

To jug a kipper, fold the sides together and place in a jug tall enough to fit the whole length of the fish. Cover with boiling water and leave to stand for 5 minutes. Pour off the water and dry the fish on a piece of kitchen paper. Serve immediately, topped with a large knob of butter.

KEDGEREE

A unique blend of Eastern and Western flavours and a remnant from England's colonial past, kedgeree is very much part of the English breakfast menu.

SERVES 4-6

The spice mix
½ teaspoon crushed
   black pepper
½ teaspoon ground coriander
½ teaspoon ground cumin
½ teaspoon ground turmeric
5 cardamom pods, crushed

5 large free-range eggs
250g/9oz basmati rice
500g/1lb 2oz undyed smoked haddock
2 bay leaves
4 black peppercorns
50g/2oz butter
1 large onion, thinly sliced
A small bunch of curly parsley, finely chopped
Salt
Lemon wedges, to serve

Boil the eggs in hot water for 12 minutes, then remove from the pan with a slotted spoon and immerse in really cold water. Peel the eggs and cut into wedges.

While the eggs are boiling combine the spices in a small bowl. Place the rice in a medium-sized pan and wash in cold water until the water runs clear. Pour off any excess water and add enough fresh cold water to cover the rice by 1cm/½ inch. Bring the rice to the boil, then reduce the heat, cover the pan and gently simmer until the rice has absorbed all the water. Turn off the heat and allow the rice to sit for 5 minutes before fluffing with a fork.

Place the smoked haddock in a large frying pan and cover with boiling water, add the bay leaves and peppercorns and gently poach for 5 minutes. Pour off the water and break the fish into bite-size chunks, discarding any rogue bones.

Heat the butter in a large non-stick frying pan. As it starts to foam add the chopped onion and cook until the onion is soft but not brown. Stir in the prepared spices and cook for a minute or so before adding the cooked rice. Combine together over a low heat until all is well mixed and nice and hot.

Gently stir in the smoked haddock and parsley, and season with salt to taste. Serve immediately topped with the boiled egg and lemon wedges.

THE PUB LUNCH

*T*he English have been making ale since the Bronze Age. Later the Romans introduced *tabernae*, offering refreshment to travellers on the new road systems that they pioneered across Britain. The Anglo-Saxons added their mark with ale houses, established in domestic dwellings in the centre of every village. Over the centuries the simple tavern grew to meet the demand for lodgings, stopping points on a long carriage journey, offering a safe place to stay and refuel before the next leg of the journey. Of course not all these establishments took the reputable route. There were those that became wretched hovels full of vice.

Over the centuries the lack of clean water supplies led to an increasing reliance on cheap gin. In 1830, in an attempt to abate the problem of drunkenness in the population, the government introduced the Beer Act, which enabled anyone to brew and sell beer on payment of a nominal licence fee. But though beer might have been a healthier option than gin, too much of a good thing can be bad for you too, and later, to discourage the huge rise in unchecked drinking dens, more expensive licences were introduced. The lucky survivors officially enlarged their repertoire, and their establishments, adding lounges and private snugs for the well-heeled, with frosted windows to hide the antics inside from the street. The public house had arrived.

The local 'pub' is now at the heart of the community, providing a meeting place to catch up on news, sup a pint of real ale and sample good honest grub. We still have a penchant for olde worlde bar snacks such as pork scratchings, rarebit and pickled eggs, the ploughman's lunch is still a satisfying midday filler, and home-made pasties and pies washed down with a pint of locally brewed beer still offer a true taste of traditional British food.

A PLOUGHMAN'S LUNCH

A ploughman's lunch is as British as roast beef and is almost guaranteed to be on the pub menu. Crusty bread, cheese, chutney and pickled onions provide a basic ploughman's, but for an exceptional lunch, choose a selection of British cheeses, cured ham carved from the bone, garden salad, proper bread, apple and home-made pickled onions and chutney.

RHUBARB AND APPLE CHUTNEY

Apple trees and rhubarb plants provide a reliable supply of produce every year in the English garden. Excess fruit is used to make chutney.

MAKES ABOUT 4 X 450G/1LB JARS
1.35kg/3lb mixed rhubarb and apples
1 largish onion, finely chopped
100ml/4floz water
400g/14oz brown sugar
1 teaspoon salt
225g/8oz raisins
1 heaped teaspoon ground ginger
1 dessertspoon grated ginger root
1 cinnamon stick or 1 teaspoon ground cinnamon
½ teaspoon cayenne pepper
1 teaspoon yellow mustard seeds
½ teaspoon crushed black pepper
425ml/¾ pint cider vinegar

Peel the rhubarb stems and peel and core the apples. Cut both into chunks.

Combine all the ingredients in a non-reactive pan and warm together over a low heat, stirring constantly until the sugar melts.

Increase the heat under the pan until a brisk simmer is reached, and continue to cook, stirring regularly, until the chutney has reduced to a jam-like consistency.

Remove the cinnamon stick and spoon the chutney into sterilized jars. Seal immediately with a tight-fitting lid. Store the chutney in a cool dark place for a couple of months before opening.

PICKLED ONIONS

England's pickle of choice!

FILLS 1 LITRE/1¾ PINT JAR
450g/1lb pickling onions
50g/2oz salt
570ml/1 pint water
425ml/¾ pint malt vinegar
2 teaspoons pickling spice

You will need a 1litre/1¾ pint jar with a tight-fitting lid

Peel the pickling onions and place them in a large bowl. Dissolve the salt in the water and pour over the onions. Cover the bowl and leave to stand for 24 hours – this ensures the pickled onions are crisp.

Pour the vinegar into a non-reactive pan, add the pickling spices and bring the vinegar to simmering point. Turn off the heat and allow the vinegar to cool.

After the allotted time, drain the onions, rinse with cold water and dab dry with a clean tea towel.

Place the onions in a sterilized 1litre/1¾ pint jar and pour the cold vinegar over the top. Seal the jar and leave for at least a month before opening.

A PIE AND A PINT

Ever since Roman times the English have heartily embraced the pie as a practical method of cooking mixed fillings over a fire or in the local bakehouse. Its virtue as an easily transportable feast helped to make it the staple diet for travellers and workers alike. And it is still going strong today as a fulfilling pub lunch with a pint of ale.

One suggestion for the derivation of the name 'pie' is that it comes from magpie – the bird famous for collecting a variety of treasures, just like the filling of a good pie!

RAISED PORK PIE

The hand-raised pork pie developed from the medieval way of making robust pastry cases or 'coffins' to protect meat during baking. The pastry would originally have been discarded, until its merits as a sturdy casing to wrap in a handkerchief for a handy packed lunch were appreciated. Originally the pastry was made from flour and water but the hot-water method was found to make a crisp tasty pastry. The pastry was filled, baked and (generally) served cold. Melton Mowbray in Leicestershire became especially famous for its pork pies.

To make the perfect raised pie pastry it must be shaped while it still hot. Traditionally, the hot pastry crust is moulded or 'raised' by hand around a wooden 'dolly'. But using a dolly is very fiddly and time-consuming. A non-stick muffin tin offers a much easier option, and is the perfect size for individual pork pies.

MAKES 6 INDIVIDUAL PIES
350g/12oz diced boneless pork
110g/4oz streaky bacon, rind
    removed and cut into strips
A good grate of nutmeg
¼ teaspoon ground mace
¼ teaspoon ground allspice
Salt and freshly ground black pepper
55ml/1floz chicken stock

The pastry
250g/9oz plain flour
A good pinch of salt
75g/3oz lard, plus extra to grease
    the tin
55ml/2oz milk
55ml/2oz water
1 beaten egg to glaze

First prepare the meat filling. Place the meat in a food processor along with the nutmeg, mace and allspice, add seasoning to taste, and blend together until the meat is roughly chopped. Add the stock and pulse the processor a couple of times.

Grease the muffin tin with a little lard and dust with a fine coating of flour. Preheat the oven to 180°C/350F/Gas mark 4.

To prepare the pastry, sift the flour and salt into a bowl and make a well in the centre. Dice the lard, place it in a pan with the milk and water, and heat together until the lard has melted and bubbles start to form around the edge of the pan.

Immediately pour the liquid into the well and quickly mix together until a dough forms. Turn the pastry out on to a floured surface and cut away a third to make the pie lids. Cut the remaining pastry into 6 equal parts and press each into the greased holes of the muffin tin until the pastry is just above the rim. Roll out the remaining pastry and cut 6 lids.

Divide the filling equally between the pastry cases. Moisten the edges with the beaten egg, place the lid on top and press the edges together until sealed. Brush the pies with beaten egg and cut a small hole in the middle. Place the tin on a baking tray and pop the pies into the oven for 35 minutes.

Remove the pies from the oven and run a blunt knife carefully around the edge. When the tin is just cool enough to touch, turn the pies out on to the baking tray. Brush the sides with beaten egg and bake for a further 20 minutes at the higher oven temperature of 190°C/375F/Gas mark 5 until golden and crisp.

PICCALILLI

This bright yellow mustardy pickle, once known as Indian pickle, shows the influence of the Empire on the traditional English method of pickling.

MAKES ABOUT 4 450G/1LB JARS

I medium cauliflower,
   cut into small florets
2 medium onions, cut into cubes
2 medium courgettes,
   cut into chunks
75g/3oz fine salt
Water to cover
3 tablespoons plain flour
3 tablespoons English mustard powder
1 tablespoon ground turmeric

850ml/1½ pint white vinegar
200g/7oz golden caster sugar
1 dessertspoon grated ginger root
¼ teaspoon cracked black pepper
¼ teaspoon ground allspice
1 dried red chilli
225g/8oz fine green beans,
   cut into quarters
½ large cucumber, peeled and diced

Start the piccalilli the day before you intend to make it. Place the cauliflower, onion and courgette in a large bowl and sprinkle evenly with the salt. Pour in enough water to cover the vegetables and leave to stand in a cool place for 24 hours. The next day drain the vegetables and rinse with cold water.

Combine the flour, mustard powder and turmeric in a small bowl and stir in a splash of the white vinegar, enough to make a thin paste. Set to one side for later.

Place the remaining vinegar in a non-reactive saucepan. Stir in the sugar and gently warm over a low heat until the sugar melts.

Add the drained vegetables, ginger, pepper, allspice and chilli. Give the pan a good stir and simmer for 10 minutes. Add the beans and cucumber and simmer for a further 5 minutes. Remove the vegetables and place in a bowl.

Whisk the flour/mustard mixture into the hot vinegar left in the pan and simmer, stirring constantly, until it is thick enough to coat the back of a spoon. Turn off the heat and return the vegetables to the pan, gently stir together until they are well coated.

Spoon the mixture into sterilised jars and seal immediately.

Store the piccalilli in a cool dark place for a couple of months before opening.

GAME PIE

Although venison and pheasant used to be strictly for the lucky few, it is a different story today. Now country pubs make the most of the abundant supply of game during the season.

SERVES 4–6

900g/2lb mix of venison steak
  and pheasant breasts
Salt and freshly ground black pepper
3 tablespoons sunflower oil
6 thick slices of streaky bacon,
  rind removed and sliced
1 large onion, cubed
2 tablespoons plain flour

150ml/¼ pint port or red wine
325ml/12floz chicken stock
1 heaped tablespoon redcurrant jelly
2 bay leaves
200g/7oz flat mushrooms, cubed
375g/13oz ready rolled puff pastry
1 small egg, beaten

Cut the venison and pheasant into cubes and season well with salt and black pepper. Heat the sunflower oil in a casserole pan (preferably cast iron), brown the meat in batches and remove from the pan with a slotted spoon.

Add the bacon and onions to the pan and cook them in the remaining oil until they are golden brown. Return the venison and pheasant to the pan, sprinkle with flour and give the pan a good stir.

Add the port (or wine) and cook at a brisk simmer, stirring constantly, until the port has reduced by half. Stir in the stock, redcurrant jelly and bay leaves, and when the redcurrant jelly has dissolved, bring the pan to the boil. Cover the pan, reduce the heat to a minimum and gently simmer for 40 minutes, adding the mushrooms after 30 minutes, and stirring the pan at regular intervals to prevent sticking.

Remove the bay leaf and spoon the mixture into a medium-sized pie dish (or individual dishes). Allow the filling to cool before covering with the pastry.

Set the oven temperature to 200°C/400F/Gas mark 6.

Brush the lip of the pie dish with beaten egg and carefully place the pastry on top, trim away any excess and firmly seal the edges. Cut a small hole in the middle and liberally brush with beaten egg.

Place the pie on a baking sheet and bake in the preheated oven for 30 minutes until the pastry is well risen and golden.

CORNISH PASTIES

The ultimate packed lunch, originally made as a filling meal for Cornish tin miners.

FOR 4 LARGE PASTIES

The pastry
450g/1lb plain flour
½ teaspoon salt
110g/4oz cold lard, diced
110g/4oz cold butter, diced
1 medium egg, beaten

The filling
350g/12oz skirt or rump steak, thinly sliced
350g/12oz waxy potatoes, thinly sliced
175g/6oz swede, thinly sliced
175g/6oz onion, finely chopped
Salt and freshly ground black pepper
Butter

Sift the flour and salt into a bowl and rub in the lard and butter until crumbs form. Gradually add enough water to form a dough, then knead the pastry for a few minutes, until it becomes elastic in texture. Wrap the pastry in cling film and place in the fridge for 30 minutes to allow it to rest.

Combine the filling ingredients in a bowl with a generous amount of seasoning – the pasties should be quite peppery.

Preheat the oven to 200°C/400F/Gas mark 6 and lightly grease a baking tray.

Cut the dough into 4 equal portions and roll out on a floured surface into circles approximately 23cm/9inches in diameter. Place a quarter of the filling in the middle of each, top with a knob of butter and brush the edges of the pastry with beaten egg. Fold the pastry over the top to make a half moon shape, crimp the edges together and brush the pasties with beaten egg.

Place the pasties on the prepared baking tray and bake for 20 minutes. Reduce the oven temperature to 180°C/350F/Gas mark 4 and continue to cook for a further 35–40 minutes, until golden brown.

ENGLISH RAREBIT

A mustardy melted cheese sauce poured over thick slices of toast soaked in red wine and grilled until bubbling hot.

SERVES 4
1 tablespoon plain flour
1 generous teaspoon English mustard powder
Pinch of cayenne pepper
6 tablespoons strong beer, dry cider or milk
1 heaped tablespoon butter
250g/9oz strong Cheddar cheese, grated
1 tablespoon Worcestershire sauce
Black pepper to taste
4 thick slices of good bread
A small glass of red wine

Combine the flour, mustard and cayenne in a bowl and gradually pour in the beer, stirring until smooth.

Place the butter in a small saucepan and melt over a low heat. Remove the pan from the heat and stir in the beer/flour mixture.

Add the cheese and gently warm, stirring constantly with a wooden spoon, until the cheese has completely melted and a thick sauce forms. Stir in the Worcestershire sauce and season to taste.

Toast the bread, sprinkle with a little red wine and spread with the cheese mixture, taking care to cover the crusts. Grill until brown and molten. Serve immediately.

OYSTERS AND STOUT

Strong, dark stout beer has had a long association with oysters. They made a popular combination in public houses and taverns throughout England from the eighteenth century, when stout was first introduced.

To prepare or shuck an oyster, you will need a short, strong shucking knife. Hold the oyster firmly with a tea towel and insert the tip of the knife at the base of the oyster shell's hinge, twist the knife, levering it upwards until the shell opens. Slide the knife under the oyster to release it from the shell, taking care not to spill any of the juices. Serve in their shells on a bed of crushed ice. A dressing of finely diced shallots combined with a little seasoned red wine vinegar makes a good accompaniment.

SAUSAGES

There was a time when most families in Britain reared a pig and pork sausages were an important part of the diet. These days your choice of sausages is not limited to pork – you can also find wild boar, venison and beef sausages, and they may be flavoured with mustard, apples, cider, fresh herbs . . . the choice is endless. Sausages from small producers and good butchers will always be best. Look for plump sausages with a high meat content. Cumberland sausages are a good bet, particularly for bangers and mash. They were originally made very long and wound into circular coils.

BANGERS, MUSTARD MASH AND ONION GRAVY

Classic pub grub at its best. Cheap, filling and, most importantly, utterly delicious. Why bangers? Well, in the past when sausages were cooked in hot fat their skins tended to split open with a bang!

SERVES 4

Onion gravy (see page 116)
8 good-quality fat sausages
Sunflower oil to fry
900g/2lb mashing potatoes,
    peeled and quartered

A large knob of butter
A good splash of milk
2 tablespoons grainy mustard

First prepare the onion gravy, following the recipe on page 116.

Place the potatoes in a saucepan, cover with water, add ½ teaspoon of salt and bring to the boil. Reduce the heat to a simmer, cover the pan and cook the potatoes until they are soft but not breaking down.

Prick the sausages and fry them until they are brown on all sides and cooked through.

Drain the potatoes, return them to the pan and heat over a lowish temperature for a minute or so, to dry off any excess water. Add the butter and milk and mash together until the potato is really smooth (whisking the mash with a hand blender makes especially fluffy mashed potato). Stir in the mustard and season to taste.

Just before serving reheat the gravy and the mash until they are piping hot, then dollop the mash onto a warm plate, spoon the gravy around the edge and place the sausages on top.

THE SUNDAY ROAST

*T*he heart of British traditional cooking, the Sunday roast provides a chance for friends and family to come together. With a plentiful supply of quality meat, the British have a long history in roasting and excel in this seemingly easy method. But there is definitely a fine art to the creation of a perfect sizzling Sunday roast, caramelized on the outside and tender inside. Timing is of the essence. So also are the famous accompaniments essential to a good roast. The humble potato comes into its own when roasted around the joint and the aroma of herby suet stuffing is wonderfully tempting. Roast lamb would seem lost without fresh mint sauce and any pork roast worth its salt needs a spoonful or two of apple sauce – and where would roast beef be without horseradish sauce and Yorkshire pudding?

Before domestic ovens came into common use, meat would be spit-roast over a fire in a large open fireplace. To ensure the meat was tender and moist, elaborate systems were invented to continually turn the joint: the simple hand crank was followed by a complex system of weights and chains, and even animal power made a brief appearance – trained dogs ran inside a wheel to keep the spit constantly turning. A dripping pan collected melting fat from the joint, and any excess dripping was collected, allowed to set and kept for future cooking. As the meat slowly turned, simple batter puddings were placed in the dripping tray to cook, catching tasty juices seeping from the meat. The pudding was served with gravy before the carved meat as a cheap, filling dish to take the edge off the appetite.

As late as the nineteenth century, while well-to-do homes would have their own ovens, most families had to make do with taking their modest Sunday roast to the local baker's to cook.

COOKING TIPS

A good roast starts with the meat. Choose the best cut you can afford and make sure it has a reasonable amount of fat – this will keep the joint moist and add lots of flavour. Dripping from a previous joint makes the best cooking fat. To make sure you have a constant supply, when you pour off excess fat from the roasting tin before making the gravy, store it in airtight container in the fridge for later use. For the best results the meat should be at room temperature when it goes in the oven, so don't take it straight from the fridge – give it some time to warm up first. For perfect beef you must take care to follow cooking times carefully (lamb and pork are a bit more forgiving). It is essential to allow the cooked joint to rest before carving; this permits the juices to be reabsorbed for a succulent roast.

ROAST BEEF, YORKSHIRE PUDDING
AND HORSERADISH SAUCE

Beef, the quintessential English Sunday roast, has always been inseparable from English cooking. Lightly cooked greens such as shredded Savoy cabbage and broccoli scattered with almonds make a healthy accompaniment or, for something more indulgent, try cauliflower cheese.

COOKING TIP

Mustard is a traditional companion to roast beef. For a delicious variation in flavour, smear the joint with English mustard at the point where the oven temperature is reduced.

ROAST BEEF

The best cuts of beef for roasting are fillet, sirloin or rib; the meat should be bright red with a good coat and marbling of fat. Beef that has been hung longer will have a fuller flavour and a slightly darker colour. A 1.5–2kg (3¼–4½lb) boned sirloin or fillet joint or a 2.5–3kg (5½–6½lb) rib joint will provide plenty of meat for 6–8 people, leaving extra for cold cuts.

Rare (red in the middle) is the traditional and most flavoursome way to serve roast beef, but this is not to every one's taste. To maximize tenderness and taste the joint should be quickly cooked, starting with a high oven temperature. Preheat the oven to 220°C/425F/Gas mark 7.

Check the weight of the beef joint and rub with a little dripping or oil. Rub the fatty surface with a sprinkling of plain flour and season with salt and freshly ground black pepper to taste. Lay the beef (fatty layer facing upwards) in a roasting tin large enough for it to sit comfortably.

Place the beef in the preheated oven for 25 minutes then reduce the oven temperature to 190°C/375F/Gas mark 5 and cook for a further 15 minutes per 450g/1lb for rare meat, 20 minutes for medium and 25 minutes for well done, basting the meat at regular intervals.

Remove the beef from the oven and transfer it to a warm serving plate. Cover with foil and a clean tea towel and leave the roast to rest for at least 20 minutes before carving. While the meat is resting, you can make the Yorkshire pudding (see page 68) and the gravy (see page 84).

YORKSHIRE PUDDING

Why Yorkshire pudding, when batter puddings are cooked all over the country? Because the Yorkshire cooking method is the best. The batter is poured into a pan of smoking hot dripping. As it hits the pan the batter sizzles and rises, creating a lighter, crisper pudding.

The traditional cooking method is described below. Alternatively, individual puddings can be made in a Yorkshire pudding tin with separate sections or a muffin tin. These smaller puddings only require 15 minutes cooking time.

SERVES 4–6

110g/4oz plain flour
2 medium free-range eggs
150ml/¼ pint whole milk

150ml/¼ pint cold water
Salt and black pepper
2 tablespoons dripping or lard

Prepare the batter when the meat goes in the oven. Sift the flour into a bowl and make a well in the centre. Beat the eggs until fluffy then whisk in the milk and water. Gradually combine the egg mixture with the flour, stirring constantly, until a smooth batter forms. Season the batter to taste and leave to stand until the beef is ready to come out of the oven.

Once the joint is removed from the oven to rest, increase the oven temperature to 220°C/425F/Gas mark 7. Pour the fat from the roasting tin into a sturdy oblong pan (approximately 28 x 18cm/11 x 7inches). When the oven is up to temperature, place the pan on the top shelf for 5 minutes or so, until the oil is smoking hot. Remove the pan from the oven, give the batter a good stir and gradually pour it into the hot pan. Put the pudding in the oven and cook for 25–30 minutes until it is golden brown and well risen.

HORSERADISH SAUCE

Hot and pungent horseradish sauce is the perfect accompaniment to roast beef, and homemade is always best.

Freshly grated horseradish root should always be the first choice, but if you find it difficult to buy the jarred option makes a good second best.

Any leftover sauce is delicious spread onto roast beef sandwiches the next day.

SERVES 4-6

2–3 tablespoons grated horseradish root
1 tablespoon white wine vinegar
150ml/¼ pint double cream

A good pinch of caster sugar
A good squeeze of lemon juice
Salt and freshly ground black pepper

Combine the grated horseradish with the white wine vinegar. Whip the double cream until it forms soft peaks and stir in the horseradish, caster sugar and a good squeeze of lemon juice. Season the sauce with salt and black pepper to taste and chill in a covered bowl in the fridge until ready to use.

ROAST PORK WITH CRACKLING, APPLE SAUCE AND STUFFING

Crunchy crackling, moist meat, sweet apple sauce and crumbly sage stuffing, classic Sunday fare. For centuries pork has snuffled its way onto the English plate.

THE ROAST PORK

Full flavoured, outdoor-reared pork always has to be the first choice, and loin or leg the most reliable cuts for a family roast. Choose meat that is firm, pink and not too fatty. Dry skin and white fat are good indications that the pig has been properly reared. A 1.5–2 kg (3¼–4½lb) boned joint will provide enough meat for 6–8 people with extra left over for cold cuts, (add an extra 450g/1lb if the joint is not boned).

For crunchy crackling it is important to prepare the skin well. Score the skin at 1cm/1½ inch intervals with a very sharp knife, taking care not to cut right through the fat to the meat. Thoroughly dry the skin with kitchen paper and generously rub medium-ground sea salt into the skin. Starting the roast off at a high temperature also gives crackling a head start, set the oven temperature to 220°C/425F/Gas mark 7.

Check the weight of the joint and place it in a roasting pan, preferably on a trivet, skin side up. Peel and quarter a red onion and tuck the chunks under the joint – the roast onion adds flavour and colour to the gravy. Leave it in the pan when you take the meat out.

Place the prepared pork in the preheated oven and roast for 30 minutes before reducing the oven temperature to 190°C/375F/Gas mark 5 and cooking the joint for a further 30 minutes per 450g/1lb of meat. Pork must be thoroughly cooked through before serving. To test the pork is cooked insert a skewer into the thickest part of the joint: the juices should run clear, if there is any pink colour to the juice return to the oven and test again.

Once cooked, place on a warmed serving plate, cover with kitchen foil and a clean tea towel and leave to rest while you prepare the gravy.

SAGE AND ONION STUFFING

Stuffing originated as yet another canny method to pad out the roast joint; breadcrumbs from leftover bread were given a makeover by mixing with suet, onion and aromatic fresh herbs. It is now inconceivable to enjoy roast pork without it.

As pork tends to be quite fatty it is best to cook the stuffing in a separate dish.

SERVES 4–6

2 large onions, finely chopped
1 smallish Bramley apple, peeled, cored and diced
A couple of generous knobs of butter, plus extra butter to grease the dish
110g/4oz home-made breadcrumbs
50g/2oz suet
1 tablespoon finely chopped sage
1 tablespoon finely chopped parsley
Salt and freshly ground black pepper
1 large free-range egg, beaten

Sauté the onion and apple in butter until soft but not brown. Allow to cool a little before combining in a bowl with the breadcrumbs, suet, sage, parsley and seasoning to taste.

Stir in the beaten egg and turn out into a buttered ovenproof dish. Place the stuffing into the oven along with the roast 10 minutes or so before the meat is cooked.

Bake in the oven for a total of 30 minutes until golden brown.

APPLE SAUCE

It was the Roman habit of serving sweet, spiced acidic fruit sauces to offset rich meat that inspired this simple apple sauce that is still inseparable from roast pork.

Prepare the sauce while the pork is cooking and reheat just before serving.

SERVES 6
450g/1lb cooking apples,
  peeled and cubed
2 generous tablespoons dry cider
1 tablespoon clear honey
½ teaspoon ground ginger and a
  good grate of nutmeg
1 heaped tablespoon butter

Gently simmer the apple, cider and honey in a small pan until the apples are soft and start to break down.

Beat in the butter, ginger and nutmeg with a wooden spoon until the sauce is smooth.

ROAST LAMB, APRICOT STUFFING AND MINT SAUCE

Tender young lamb always makes a reliable, tasty, no-fuss roast. Homemade acidic fresh mint sauce cuts through the lamb fat to create a marriage made in heaven.

Young British lamb is at its absolute best in spring, making it a top choice for an Easter Sunday roast.

THE ROAST LAMB

Choose a joint with pink firm flesh and white fat. Leg and shoulder are the prime cuts. Shoulder tends to be more fatty and can be cooked either on the bone or boned and rolled. A 1.5–2 kg (3¼–4½lb) boned joint will provide enough meat for 6–8 people, with extra for cold cuts (add an extra 450g/1lb if the joint is not boned). The rich musty meat is enhanced when cooked with strong-flavoured herbs such as thyme and rosemary.

To satisfy all tastes a lamb joint should ideally be cooked pink in the middle with well done crunchy ends. Check the weight of the joint, rub the skin with a little olive oil and season with sea salt and freshly ground pepper to taste. Place the lamb in a roasting tin and tuck a peeled onion cut into quarters underneath to add extra flavour to the gravy. Pop the lamb into an oven preheated to 200°C/400F/Gas mark 6. Calculate the cooking time based on 20 minutes per 450g/1lb plus an extra 20 minutes. If you prefer your lamb less pink in the middle, allow 25 minutes per 450g/1lb plus an extra 25 minutes.

COOKING TIPS

You can't beat lamb cooked with rosemary and garlic. For a 2kg/4½lb prepared joint, slice 4 garlic cloves into slivers, make small, deep cuts in the meat with the point of a sharp knife, and insert the slivers into the cuts along with a few rosemary leaves.

A boned shoulder joint is good rolled with thyme and honey. For a 2kg/4½lb joint, open the meat, lay it skin side down, sprinkle with 2 tablespoon of fresh thyme leaves, drizzle with 2 tablespoon clear honey, season to taste, roll and secure with string tied at regular intervals. Roast the rolled joint in the usual way.

APRICOT STUFFING

The fruity sweetness of dried apricots has for centuries made them a popular accompaniment to roast lamb; the stuffing can either be cooked rolled inside a boned shoulder joint, or placed around the meat.

SERVES 4–6
1 large onion, diced
3 generous tablespoons butter
150g/5oz homemade breadcrumbs
175g/6oz ready-to-eat dried apricots, diced
1 tablespoon chopped thyme
1 dessertspoon chopped rosemary
The grated zest and juice of a lemon
Salt and black pepper

Fry the diced onion in 2 tablespoons of the butter until it is soft but not brown. Add the remaining butter and stir in the breadcrumbs and apricots until they are well coated. Turn off the heat and add the herbs, lemon juice and seasoning to taste.

To stuff the shoulder joint, open the meat and lay it skin side down, place the stuffing in the middle and roll the sides around the stuffing. Secure the joint with string tied at regular intervals, season to taste and roast in the normal way – making sure to take into account the stuffing weight when calculating cooking times.

Alternatively add the stuffing to the roasting pan 30 minutes before the joint is ready.

MINT SAUCE

The Romans were partial to cooking with herbs and arrived in England with a plentiful supply to cultivate. Fresh mint was pickled in vinegar and sweetened with honey – all in all not very different from the classic sweet and sour mint sauce served with lamb today.

SERVES 4–6
4 tablespoons finely chopped mint leaves
1 tablespoon caster sugar dessert
4 tablespoons white wine vinegar

Combine the chopped mint with the sugar in a small bowl.
Add the vinegar and stir until the sugar has dissolved to make a thin sauce.

POTATOES

The British love affair with the potato first began in the late sixteenth century when Sir Walter Raleigh returned triumphantly to England from the Americas carrying this exotic prize to the table of Queen Elizabeth I. Initially the potato was viewed with distrust outside court – some even thought it was poisonous. Eventually the potato became accepted as an easy to cultivate food staple, downgrading its status as a highly prized vegetable to being considered food for the poor. It wasn't until the late nineteenth century, with the influence of recipes from Europe and a larger choice of varieties, that the potato became universally accepted as a valuable ingredient.

ROAST POTATOES

Potatoes can be cooked around the meat or in a separate roasting tin. Cooked around the meat they absorb the meat juices, whereas if they are cooked separately they are crunchier on the outside. Duck fat makes superb roast potatoes, as does dripping, but if you prefer a lighter option stick to sunflower oil.

SERVES 6
1.35kg/3lb floury potatoes
5 tablespoons goose fat, dripping, or sunflower oil
Salt

Peel the potatoes and cut into largish chunks. Parboil the chunks for around 5 minutes in boiling water, drain them well, return to the pan and steam dry for a minute or so over a low heat, shaking the pan as you do so.

Approximately 1 hour before the meat is cooked add the cooking oil of your choice to a roasting tin big enough to fit the potatoes in a single layer. Place the pan in the oven for 5 or so minutes until it is smoking hot. Add the potatoes and toss them in the fat until they are well coated, then season with salt to taste. Return the pan to the oven and cook the potatoes for an hour and a quarter or so, until they are brown and crunchy, turning them a couple of times to prevent them sticking, and ensuring they are equally roasted on all sides.

Once the meat has been removed from the oven lower the oven temperature to a medium temperature to keep the roast potatoes warm while you prepare the gravy and rest the meat.

If you are cooking the potatoes around the joint, add the parboiled potatoes to the roasting pan approximately 1 hour 15 minutes before the meat is cooked. Coat with the hot oil in the roasting pan, season with salt and cook using the same method as above.

VEG

Meat and two veg, the backbone of British cookery. Here is a selection of the very best vegetables to serve with a Sunday roast.

CLAPSHOT

Buttery mashed swede and potato soaks up savoury gravy perfectly. Clapshot is thought to have originated in the Orkney Islands but is now popular throughout Britain.

The swede or yellow turnip first appeared in the royal gardens in the seventeenth century. An exotic import from Europe, it grew well in England and soon became commonplace, even providing fodder for animals through the winter months.

The water drained from the cooked vegetables can be reserved and used to make the gravy. If you are serving your joint with roast potatoes, you can replace the potato in clapshot with the same quantity of cooked carrots if you prefer.

SERVES 4–6
450g/1lb swede, peeled and cut into large chunks
450g/1lb floury potatoes (or carrots), peeled and cut into large chunks
110g/4oz butter
5 tablespoons double cream
Salt and freshly ground black pepper
A dessertspoon chopped chives

Cook the swede and potato in salted boiling water until soft.

Drain the vegetables, return to the pan and add the butter, cream and seasoning to taste. Mash together until smooth, then beat with a wooden spoon or hand whisk until creamy.

Finally stir in the chopped chives.

ROAST VEGETABLES

Parsnips are indigenous to Britain and before the arrival of sugar were often used as a sweetening agent in recipes; their hardy nature made the parsnip an important staple in British cookery. Mixed with carrots and swede and roasted until golden, they make an irresistible side dish to any roast.

SERVES 6
5 generous tablespoons olive oil
4 medium parsnips, peeled and cut into equal sized chunks
3 carrots, peeled and quartered lengthwise
⅓ medium swede, peeled and cut into chunks
1 largish red onion, peeled and cut into chunks
6 garlic cloves, unpeeled
3 stalks of rosemary, leaves removed
A good grate of nutmeg
Salt and black pepper

Pour the olive oil into a roasting tin large enough to fit the vegetables in a single layer, place the tin in the oven with the joint approximately 35 minutes before the end of the roasts calculated cooking time. After 5 minutes, when the oil is really hot, remove the tin from the oven.

Add the prepared vegetables and turn them in the hot oil until well coated. Arrange the vegetables in a single layer and season with salt and freshly ground black pepper to taste.

Return to the oven and cook for 30 minutes, before sprinkling with the rosemary leaves and grated nutmeg. Continue to cook the vegetables in the oven for a further 30 minutes or so until golden brown.

SPICED BRAISED RED CABBAGE

By the sixteenth century new varieties of cabbage, first introduced to Britain by the Romans, began to be developed. Red cabbage quickly became popular. It was usually cooked slowly with spices and fruit and served with roast meats. It is particularly good with pork and turkey.

SERVES 4–6
500g/1lb 2oz thinly sliced red cabbage
1 medium red onion, thinly sliced
2 medium-sized tart apples, cored and sliced
A handful of dried raisins
8 cloves
8 allspice berries
A good grate of nutmeg
2 tablespoons butter plus extra to butter the dish
1 tablespoon clear honey
Salt and freshly ground black pepper
3 tablespoons cider vinegar
150ml/¼ pint apple juice

Layer the sliced red cabbage, apple, red onion and raisins in a buttered ovenproof casserole dish. Sprinkle the spices on top, dot with butter and drizzle with honey. Season to taste and pour the vinegar and apple juice evenly over the top.

Cover the dish and place in the oven with the joint for 1½ hours or so, until the cabbage is soft and cooked down. The cover should be removed for the last ½ hour of cooking time.

CAULIFLOWER CHEESE

Creamy and cheesy, a tried and true favourite with any roast.

SERVES 6
1 medium cauliflower
40g/1½oz butter
40g/1½oz plain flour
275ml/½ pint whole milk
150g/5oz strong Cheddar cheese, grated
1 teaspoon English mustard powder
Salt and black pepper

Cut the cauliflower into largish florets and cook in salted water until just soft. Drain the cauliflower well, reserving 150ml/¼ pint of the cooking water as you do so.

Melt the butter in a saucepan, stir in the flour and cook the resulting roux for a minute or so, stirring constantly. Remove the pan from the heat and whisk in the milk and the cauliflower water. Return the pan to the heat and gently cook, stirring constantly, until the sauce thickens. Add three-quarters of the grated cheese and stir together until the cheese has melted. Add the mustard and season to taste.

Place the cauliflower in a heatproof dish, pour the sauce evenly over the top and sprinkle with the remaining cheese.

Place in the hot oven 15 minutes before the roast is ready to come out. Bake for 30 minutes until golden brown. Lower the heat to a minimum to keep the cauliflower cheese hot until ready to serve.

GLAZED CARROTS WITH FRESH CHERVIL

Carrots, considered so English, are in fact native to Arabia. As the Arabs colonised southern Spain carrots were cultivated and by the sixteenth century made their way to England.

The ancient method of braising the carrots with oil and wine intensifies the carrots sweetness.

SERVES 4–6
775g/1lb 10oz carrots
50g/2oz butter
100ml/4floz dry white wine
100ml/4floz hot vegetable stock
Salt and freshly ground black pepper
2 tablespoons finely chopped chervil or parsley

Peel the carrots, cut in half and cut into finger shaped pieces. Melt the butter in a heavy saucepan and add the carrots, turning them in the butter until well coated.

Pour in the wine and stock, add seasoning to taste and gently simmer in the covered pan until the carrots start to soften.

Remove the lid and continue to simmer until the liquid has reduced and the carrots are glazed and soft but still retaining a little bite.

Combine the carrots with the chopped chervil and serve in a warmed dish.

NO-NONSENSE CHRISTMAS TURKEY ROAST

Christmas is inconceivable without a plump turkey roast. The buxom bird has been synonymous with Christmas since the sixteenth century when it first arrived on Britain's shores from the Americas. Henry VIII decided he preferred the full-flavoured bird to peacock or swan and heralded the turkey as his bird of choice for feast days. Huge flocks of turkey were walked from East Anglia to the teaming streets of London, a journey that could take up to three months.

Now we are lucky enough to have a wide choice in the type of turkeys available. Taste and texture have to be number one priority. Slowly reared, mature, free-range birds are full of flavour compared to their intensively reared counterpart. A fresh bird makes a much more successful roast than frozen, which will inevitably have extra added water to the meat.

A 4.5kg/10lb bird will feed 6–8 comfortably with enough extra meat left over for Boxing Day sandwiches.

Stick to a few basic rules and you will achieve a stress free festive feast with the minimum amount of fuss.

- Always ensure the turkey is at room temperature before it goes in the oven – take the bird out of the fridge just before bedtime for lunch or first thing in the morning for dinner. Store the bird in a cool place until you are ready to prepare it.

- Make sure you add extra wide kitchen foil to your Christmas shopping list.

- Most turkeys will come with giblets tucked inside the turkey cavity encased in a small plastic bag. These are traditionally used to make stock for the gravy. Always double-check you've taken the bag out before putting the bird in the oven! To make turkey stock, place the giblets in a pan with a peeled and quartered onion, a couple of bay leaves and a few sprigs of thyme. Pour 1 litre/1¾ pints of water over the top, cover the pan and gently simmer for 45 minutes. Strain the stock into a jug ready to make the gravy.

- Cocktail sausages wrapped in streaky bacon are a must. Allow approximately 3 per person and always choose good-quality baby sausages and dry-cured bacon. Cut away the bacon rind, stretch each rasher by running the blunt edge of a knife along its length and wrap the 'stretched' bacon tightly around each sausage.

- Cook roast potatoes in a separate roasting tin - there really isn't enough room for both!

- Cauliflower cheese and braised red cabbage are excellent vegetable accompaniments (see pages 93, 92), but don't forget the Brussels sprouts! Simmer peeled Brussels sprouts in salted water until they are just soft, drain well and set to one side. Fry sliced back bacon (about one smallish slice per person) in a little olive oil until crispy. Add a generous knob of butter and as it starts to melt add the drained Brussels. Season with freshly ground black pepper and a good grating of nutmeg. Gently turn the Brussels until they are coated with all the lovely flavours.

- For succulent meat with a crispy brown skin, begin and end roasting the bird at a higher temperature.

LET'S GET STARTED!
To simplify things, prepare the stuffing and the cranberry sauce the day before . . .

CHESTNUT STUFFING

SERVES 6–8

200g/7oz ready-peeled chestnuts
2 tablespoons butter
1 large onion, finely diced
110g/4oz streaky bacon,
    rind removed and thinly sliced
150g/5oz homemade breadcrumbs

75g/3oz suet
2 tablespoons finely chopped parsley
1 tablespoon finely chopped thyme
Grated zest of a large lemon
Salt and freshly ground black pepper
    to taste

Simmer the chestnuts in salted boiling water for 15 minutes or so, until they are soft. Drain, rinse with cold water and roughly chop in a food processor.

Fry the onion and bacon in butter until they are cooked through but not brown. Stir in the chestnuts and continue to cook for a couple of minutes. Allow to cool a little before combining with the remaining ingredients. Store in the fridge until required.

CRANBERRY SAUCE

This tart spiced sauce is a Christmas essential. Make sure there is enough left over to spread cold onto turkey sandwiches.

SERVES 6–8

350g/12oz fresh or
   frozen cranberries
75g/3oz–110g/4oz soft brown sugar
Juice and zest of a large orange

A splash of port (optional)
1 small cinnamon stick
½ teaspoon ground mace
Freshly ground black pepper

Place all the ingredients in a saucepan and simmer together until the cranberries 'pop' and start to break down. Crush a few of the berries with the back of a spoon on the side of the pan to thicken the sauce. Remove the cinnamon stick and allow the sauce to cool to room temperature before serving – the sauce will thicken slightly as it cools.

THE GRAVY

Follow the recipe for gravy on page 84, adding a small glass of dry red or white wine to the juices and reducing the wine by half before adding 850ml/1½ pint of giblet (or chicken) stock mixed with a rounded tablespoon of plain flour thinned with a little water. A dessertspoon or two of redcurrant jelly is also rather good stirred into the gravy.

THE TURKEY

4.5 kilo/10lb free-range turkey
110g/4oz soft butter
2 medium onions, quartered

Salt and freshly ground black pepper
12 rashers of streaky bacon,
rind removed

Place the lower oven shelf at the bottom and preheat to 220°C/425F/Gas mark 7.

Lay 2 lengths of extra-wide foil at right angles to each other in the bottom of the roasting tin – make sure the foil is cut long enough to loosely cover the turkey.

Remove the giblets from the turkey and place the bird in the middle of the foil. Rub the soft butter over its skin and season well with salt and black pepper.

Lightly pack the stuffing inside the neck cavity of the turkey (any extra can be cooked in a separate buttered dish), fold the skin over the top and secure with a cocktail stick. Lay the streaky bacon across the top of the turkey.

Tuck the chopped onions underneath the turkey and fold the foil loosely over the turkey, leaving enough room for steam to circulate.

Place the turkey on the lowered shelf in the oven and cook for 30 minutes before reducing the temperature to 180°C/350F/Gas mark 4 and continuing to cook for 2½ hours.

Remove the turkey from the oven and increase the oven temperature to 220°C/425F/Gas mark 7. Open up the foil to completely uncover the turkey and baste well. Return to the oven and cook for a further 20–25 minutes, until the skin is golden brown and crisp.

To check the turkey is cooked through, insert a skewer into the thickest part of the leg. The juices must run clear – if in doubt, return the turkey to the oven, cook for a further 15 minutes and test again.

Lift the turkey out of the pan on to a warmed carving plate, cover with a new sheet of foil and a clean tea towel and allow to rest for 30 minutes before carving.

THE NATION'S FAVOURITES

*T*he origins of many of Britain's most-loved dishes can be traced back over centuries. They represent a cultural mishmash of ingredients borrowed from Britain's invaders, trading partners and neighbours, stirred together with a large measure of home-grown flavours and a generous pinch of making do. A large number of England's favourite recipes are the happy consequence of creative cooks inventing devilish ways to make a little go a long way; the tasty yet frugal batter in toad-in-the-hole bridges the gap, leaving just enough room for a modest serving of sausage.

Limited cooking methods have also played a fair part in shaping Britain's most enjoyable dishes. Until relatively recently an open fire was the only cooking device in the home, giving rise to cauldron cookery and tasty tender stews garlanded with dumplings, and the easily transportable one pot Lancashire hotpot. Later innovations in kitchen gadgetry put sumptuous steamed puddings on the plate and proper pies in the oven; hearty recipes that appealed to English taste buds and tummies.

Monarchs and their foreign spouses added glamour and fashionable trends to the table, Charles I's wife, Henrietta Maria of France, famously injected a little 'je ne sais quoi' into English cookery when she arrived with her favourite chefs from home. England's colourful and varied history of empire and immigration has enriched the English diet no end, while 'foreign' delicacies such as good old fish and chips have been enthusiastically assimilated into English cuisine to become top of the roll call of the nation's favourite dishes.

LANCASHIRE HOTPOT

Named after the pottery dish in which the slow-cooked casserole was originally prepared, Lancashire hotpot came about in the Lancashire mill towns in the nineteenth century.

SERVES 4–6

2 tablespoons sunflower oil
8 best end neck of lamb chops
4 lamb's kidneys, core removed
  and sliced
2 medium onions, thinly sliced
900g/2lb waxy potatoes,
  peeled and thinly sliced

2 sprigs rosemary
3 bay leaves
Salt and freshly ground black pepper
425ml/¾ pint hot lamb
  or vegetable stock
Butter

Preheat the oven to 180C/350F/Gas mark 4

Heat the oil in a large frying pan and when it is sizzling hot brown the lamb and kidneys in batches. Remove the meat from the pan, add the onion and cook in the meat juices until it starts to soften.

Grease a deep casserole dish (with a fitted lid) with a generous coating of butter and lay half the potato slices across the bottom, overlapping the slices as you do so.

Cover the potatoes with half the onions and season with salt and black pepper to taste.

Place the meat on top and season once more. Strip the rosemary leaves from the stalk and sprinkle over the meat. Add the bay leaves and pour over the hot stock.

Cover the casserole with the remaining potatoes (using the same overlapping method), dot with butter and add a final seasoning of salt and pepper.

Cover the casserole with a lid (or kitchen foil) and place in the preheated oven for 2 hours, removing the lid for the last half-hour. If you like the potatoes to be really crunchy, place the casserole under a hot grill for a further 5 minutes.

SHEPHERD'S PIE

Shepherd's pie is thought to have originated in the North of England, where sheep-farming was common, as a thrifty way of using up left over roast lamb. The pie can be made in one big dish or individual portions.

SERVES 4–6

900g/2lb mashing potatoes,
  peeled and cut into chunks
3 tablespoons single cream
  or whole milk
2 heaped tablespoons butter
Salt and freshly ground black pepper
2 tablespoons lard or butter
1 large onion, diced
2 cloves crushed garlic
2 carrots, diced

375g/13oz leftover cooked lamb,
  minced or finely chopped
1 tablespoon plain flour
2 heaped tablespoons tomato purée
A good shake of Worcestershire sauce
225ml/8floz lamb stock
1 dessertspoon chopped thyme
1 tablespoon chopped parsley
Salt and freshly ground black pepper
Butter to grease the dish

First prepare the mashed potato: cook the potatoes in simmering salted water until they are soft but not breaking down. Drain the potatoes and return to the pan to steam dry over a low heat for a minute or so, shaking the pan constantly to prevent sticking. Add the cream and butter and mash together until the potato is really smooth. Season to taste with extra salt and freshly ground black pepper, cover the pan and set to one side

Heat two-thirds of the lard in a large frying pan, add the onion, garlic and carrot and cook until soft.

Remove the vegetables from the pan, add the remaining lard and when the fat has melted and is sizzling hot, brown the meat.

Return the vegetables to the pan along with the meat and stir in the flour, tomato purée and Worcestershire sauce until well combined.

Add the stock, chopped herbs and seasoning to taste and give the pan a good stir. Simmer together for 5 minutes or so until the gravy thickens.

Preheat the oven to 190°C/375F/Gas mark 5 and butter a largish pie or casserole dish.

Spoon the lamb filling into the prepared pie dish and cover with the mashed potato. Using the back of a fork level the potato, drawing furrows with the prongs across the top.

Liberally dot the potato with butter, place on a baking tray, and bake in the preheated oven for 25–30 minutes until golden brown (if making individual pies 20 minutes is plenty).

THE SAVOURY PUDDING

Savoury puddings have been cooked in England for centuries, but it was the invention of the muslin pudding cloth in the seventeenth century that enabled puddings to be made all year round. Previously puddings were limited to the autumn pudding season when animals were slaughtered before the winter and the intestines used to contain the pudding. The completed pudding would be wrapped in the special muslin cloth and its ends gathered on top and tied together making the characteristic round shape. Then it would be left to bubble away for hours in simmering water or stock until cooked. Eventually the pudding basin eclipsed the cloth as a much easier method.

COOK'S TIP

Make the filling a day in advance. The flavours improve as they mature and a little time to settle makes assembling the pudding much easier.

You can also use the steak and kidney recipe from the following pages as a pie filling. Cook the casserole in the oven for the slightly longer time of 1½ hours. Allow it to cool before spooning into a pie dish with a wide lip. Brush the lip with beaten egg and cover with 450g/1lb ready-rolled puff pastry. Lightly prick the pastry with a fork, cut a small hole in the middle and brush with beaten egg.

Bake the pie in an oven preheated to 200°C/400F/Gas mark 6, until the pastry is golden brown and puffed up.

STEAK AND KIDNEY PUDDING

Although England has a long history of steak puddings, adding kidney is a relatively new variation. Steak puddings were often padded out with cheap oysters, but as oysters became less plentiful and more expensive, kidneys took their place.

Traditionally the pudding is served spooned from the bowl. As it is quite filling, the only thing needed to accompany it is some lightly cooked green vegetables.

SERVES 4–6

560g/1lb 4oz stewing steak
250g/9oz lambs kidneys
2 tablespoons dripping,
    lard or sunflower oil
1 medium onion, diced
2 tablespoons plain flour
275ml/½ pint good beef stock
275ml/½ pint stout
A small bunch of thyme
2 bay leaves

A good shake of Worcestershire sauce
Salt and freshly ground black pepper

The suet pastry
275g/10oz self-raising flour
150/5oz suet
½ teaspoon salt
Water to mix
Butter to grease the pudding bowl and
    the greaseproof paper

Preheat the oven to 180°C/350F/Gas mark 4.

Cut the stewing steak into bite-size cubes and season with salt. Cut the kidneys in half, remove the white core and cut into slightly smaller cubes, season with salt.

Heat half the lard in a casserole pan and fry the onions until soft. Remove the onions from the pan with a slotted spoon, add the remaining lard and, when it is sizzling hot, brown the meat in batches.

Return the onion to the pan along with the meat and sprinkle with flour. Stir well and pour in the stock and stout. Add the herbs and a good shake of Worcestershire sauce and, using a wooden spoon, scrape the meaty bits from the bottom of the pan.

Season with salt and black pepper to taste and bring the pan to the boil. Cover the casserole with a lid, place in the preheated oven and cook for 1 hour. Allow the meat to cool before removing the thyme and bay leaves.

To make the pastry, combine the self-raising flour, suet and salt in a mixing bowl and gradually add enough water to make a soft dough. Reserve a quarter of the pastry to make the pudding lid and set to one side. Roll out the remaining three-quarters on a floured surface until it is roughly ½cm/¼ inch thick and large enough in diameter to fill the pudding bowl.

Generously butter a 1.2 litre/2 pint heatproof pudding bowl and carefully line with the rolled out pastry, taking care not to stretch the pastry. Fill the pudding with the cooled steak and kidney mixture, making sure it comes to approximately 2cm/¾ inch below the top of the pastry. Place any excess gravy in a small pan to serve hot alongside the pudding.

Roll out the remaining pastry until it snuggly covers the filling. Lay the lid on top of the pudding, damp the edges with water and fold the pastry sides over the top, gently pressing the edges together as you do so to ensure a good seal.

Cover the pudding bowl with kitchen foil lined with a sheet of buttered greaseproof paper (butter side down), making sure they are cut large enough to fold a 4cm/1½ inch pleat down the middle (to allow the pudding to rise) and have enough overhang to tie a length of string around the edge to secure it. Cut the string long enough to tie a handle on top – it is a great help when lifting the pudding in and out of the pan.

Place the pudding in a saucepan with a trivet or folded tea towel in the bottom and add enough boiling water to come half way up the side of the bowl. Cover the pan with a tight fitting lid and gently simmer the pudding for 2 hours, topping up with extra boiling water if necessary.

Carefully lift the pudding from the pan, allow it to sit for 15 minutes before removing the foil cover. Slide a blunt palate knife around the edge and turn out onto a large plate (alternatively spoon the pudding directly from the bowl), serve thick slices topped with the heated reserved gravy.

TOAD-IN-THE-HOLE AND RED ONION GRAVY

Originally this dish was made with leftover cuts of meat, a delicious method of making a little go a long way. It is now commonly agreed that the name must have been suggested by the sight of the cooked meat peeping out of the fluffy browned batter and looking rather like a toad.

SERVES 4–6

8 good-quality fat sausages
1 tablespoon dripping or lard

The batter
175g/6oz plain flour
3 medium free-range eggs, beaten
425ml/¾ pint mix of equal quantities
  of full-fat milk and cold water
Salt and freshly ground black pepper

The gravy
1 tablespoon sunflower oil
1 heaped tablespoon butter
2 medium red onions, thinly sliced
A couple of sprigs of rosemary
560ml/1 pint vegetable stock
1 heaped tablespoon redcurrant jelly
1 rounded teaspoon plain flour, dissolved
  in a little water to make a thin paste
Salt and freshly ground black pepper

Preheat the oven to 220°C/425F/Gas mark 7.

Sift the flour into a bowl, make a well in the centre, add the eggs and beat the flour and eggs together until they are well incorporated. Gradually beat in the milk, crushing any lumps on the side of the bowl, until a smooth batter forms. Season the batter to taste and allow to stand while you prepare the gravy.

Heat the sunflower oil and butter in a frying pan. When the butter starts to foam, add the onion and rosemary, cover the pan and cook on a low heat until the onions are really soft but not brown. Stir in the stock and redcurrant jelly and when the jelly has dissolved add the flour water. Gently simmer together until the gravy thickens.

Place the lard in a medium-sized roasting tin. Pop the tin in the preheated oven until the lard melts. Remove the tin from the oven, lay the sausages in the hot fat, return to the oven and cook for 10 minutes.

Give the batter a quick stir, remove the pan from the oven once more, evenly space the sausages and quickly pour the batter around them. Immediately return the pan to the oven and cook for a further 30 minutes, until the Yorkshire pudding is golden brown and well risen.

Cut into portions and serve smothered with onion gravy.

DUMPLINGS

In Norfolk, dumplings, fashioned from little balls of dough left over from the day's bread-making, were steamed on top of savoury stews – a useful way to make a meal go further. Suet mixed with flour was found to make a light fluffy dumpling and herbs, grated horseradish or chopped dried fruit added depth of flavour to the dish.

BEEF, OYSTER AND MUSHROOM STEW
WITH HERB DUMPLINGS

Simple slow-cooked one-pot stews cooked over a fire in a cauldron were the original mainstay of English cuisine. If you are not fond of oysters add a few extra mushrooms.

SERVES 4–6

2 tablespoons butter
10 shallots, peeled and left whole
5 thick slices of streaky bacon,
    rind removed and sliced
2 tablespoons sunflower oil
750g/1lb 10oz cubed stewing steak
350ml/12floz beer
350ml/12floz good beef stock
3 carrots cut into chunks
Small bunch of thyme
Small handful finely chopped
    curly parsley
6 juniper berries
1 tablespoon mushroom ketchup
Salt and freshly ground black pepper

6 oysters removed from their shells
200g/6oz brown cap button mushrooms
2 tablespoons plain flour and 1 teaspoon
    mustard powder mixed with enough
    water to make a thin paste

The dumplings

150g/5oz self-raising flour
60g/2½ oz suet
2 tablespoons finely chopped
    curly parsley
1 tablespoon finely chopped sage
Salt and freshly ground black pepper
Water

Heat the butter in a largish casserole pan. As the butter stars to foam, add the shallots and bacon and fry until golden brown. Remove the shallots and bacon from the pan with a slotted spoon and set to one side.

Add the sunflower oil to the same pan, and when sizzling hot, brown the stewing steak in batches, adding extra oil if necessary.

Return the shallots and bacon to the casserole along with the browned meat, add the beer and stock and give the pan a good stir with a wooden spoon, scraping the caramelized bits from the bottom of the pan.

Add the carrots, herbs, juniper berries and mushroom ketchup. Season to taste and bring the stew to the boil. Reduce the heat, cover the pan and simmer for 1 hour 10 minutes, stirring occasionally to prevent the stew sticking.

Meanwhile make the herb dumplings. Combine the flour, suet, chopped parsley and sage and seasoning to taste, and gradually stir in enough water to make a sticky dough. Divide the dough into 6 portions, coat in flour and roll each portion into round balls.

After 1 hour 10 minutes add the oysters and button mushrooms and stir in the flour/mustard water. Carefully position the dumplings evenly spaced on top, cover the pan and simmer for a further 30 minutes, until the gravy is thick, the meat tender and the dumplings light and fluffy,

CHICKEN AND MUSHROOM PIE

Cream became an important ingredient in recipes from the south-west of England, where cattle-farming was prevalent.

SERVES 4–6

110g/4oz plain flour
110g/4oz self-raising flour
Pinch of salt
110g/4oz butter or equal quantities
   of butter and lard, diced
Water to bind
4 skinless free-range chicken thighs
2 skinless free-range chicken breasts
Olive oil
1 heaped tablespoon butter,
   plus extra to butter the pie dish
1 medium onion, diced

1 garlic clove, finely chopped
1 medium leek, cleaned and sliced
175g/6oz brown cap mushrooms,
   cut into chunks
1 heaped tablespoon plain flour
½ teaspoon ground mace
200ml/7floz double cream
100ml/4floz chicken stock
1 dessertspoon chopped tarragon
1 tablespoon chopped parsley
Salt and freshly ground black pepper
1 small free-range egg, beaten

Sift the flour and salt into a bowl and rub in the butter and lard until crumbs form. Be careful not to over-handle the mixture at this stage or the pastry will become hard. Gradually add enough water to bring the pastry together. Shape the pastry into a ball, cover with cling film and allow to rest in the fridge while you prepare the filling.

Remove the thigh meat from the bone and cut into chunks. Cut the breast meat into thickish strips. Season the prepared chicken with a little salt and brown in a large frying pan with a generous splash of olive oil. Remove the chicken from the pan with a slotted spoon and set to one side.

Add the butter to the same pan and sauté the onion, garlic and leeks until they start to soften. Add the mushrooms and cook for a further couple of minutes.

Return the chicken to the pan and sprinkle with the plain flour and mace. Give the pan a good stir and pour in the cream and stock. Gently simmer together for a few minutes, stirring constantly, until the sauce thickens. Add the chopped herbs and seasoning to taste and spoon into a medium pie dish. Set to one side to cool.

Preheat the oven to 190°C/375F/Gas mark 5.

When the filling has cooled roll out the pastry to the correct size to fit comfortably on top of the pie dish. Brush the lip of the dish with beaten egg and lay the pastry on top. Cut away any excess pastry and firmly crimp the edge. Brush with beaten egg and cut a couple of slits in the centre to allow steam to escape.

Place the pie on a baking tray and bake in the preheated oven for 40 minutes until golden brown.

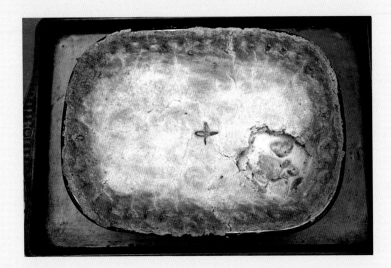

FISH AND CHIPS

The original 'pescado frito' dates back to the seventeenth century, when Jewish immigrants from Spain and Portugal started to peddle battered fish cooked in huge cauldrons of boiling oil as a street snack.

By the mid-nineteenth century trawl fishing in the North Sea provided a plentiful supply of fresh fish that, via a new network of railway lines, could be quickly transported to the city markets.

The tasty and nutritious battered fish provided light relief from the monotony of many a mill and factory worker's diet. Sales soared and to meet the demand numerous businesses set up shop, adding chips to the menu to provide a more substantial supper, wrapping them all together in newspaper to keep the cost down.

BEER-BATTERED COD AND TWICE-COOKED CHIPS

For crispy batter and crunchy chips every time, ensure the oil is always up to the desired temperature and cook the fish and chips in batches, only half filling the pan.

Twice-frying the prepared potatoes guarantees chips that are soft and fluffy on the inside and crisp on the outside. A food thermometer is essential to measure the correct temperature (and always remember to take great care when working with hot oil).

For a true taste of England sprinkle with a good shake of salt and vinegar and serve with tartare sauce, mushy or fresh peas, and slices of bread and butter.

SERVES 4

The chips
4 largish floury potatoes, peeled

The beer batter
110g/4oz self-raising flour
50g/2oz cornflour
200ml/7floz pint good beer
Salt

The fish
4 x 200g/7oz chunky fillets of skinless cod or haddock (pollock makes a good ethical alternative)
4 tablespoons plain flour seasoned to taste with salt

Sunflower oil to deep fry

Cut the potatoes into 1cm/½ inch chunky chips. To remove the starch wash the chips in cold running water until the water runs clear. Soak the washed chips in cold water while you prepare the batter.

Sift the two flours into a bowl and make a well in the centre. Gradually pour the ale into the well, whisking constantly as you do so, and crushing any lumps on the side of the bowl, until the batter is smooth and thick enough to coat the back of a wooden spoon. Season with salt to taste and leave to rest while you cook the chips.

Half-fill a deep-fat fryer or heavy bottomed medium-sized pan (with a wire basket) with sunflower oil and heat the oil to 140°C/275F.

Drain the chips and thoroughly dry in a clean tea towel – it is important that the chips are completely dry. Place half the chips in the basket and lower into the hot oil.

Cook for 6–8 minutes, until soft but not brown. Remove the chips and drain on kitchen paper while you fry the remaining potatoes. Place the part-cooked chips in a warm oven while you cook the fish.

Place the wire basket in the pan and heat the oil to the higher temperature of 190°C/375F.

Lightly coat two fish fillets with the seasoned flour and dip into the batter. When the fillets are well coated, place in the basket and lower into the preheated oil. Cook for 6–8 minutes (depending on the thickness of the fish) until the batter is golden brown and crisp. Lift the fish from the oil and drain on kitchen paper while you fry the remaining fillets. Place the battered fish in the warm oven while you finish cooking the chips.

Reheat the oil to 190°C/375F and cook the chips in two batches until crisp and brown on the outside. This should take around 3 minutes depending on how brown you like your chips.

MUSHY PEAS

Mushy peas are the traditional accompaniment to fish and chips, but they are quite an acquired taste. Feel free to serve with fresh peas if you prefer.

225g/8oz dried marrowfat peas, soaked overnight in cold water
1 medium onion, finely diced
2 heaped tablespoons butter

1 teaspoon finely chopped mint leaves (optional)
Salt and freshly ground black pepper

Drain the peas and rinse well. Tip into a pan and add the diced onion.

Add enough water to just cover the peas and simmer until the peas start to break down and have absorbed most of the water.

Beat in the butter and add the chopped mint and seasoning to taste.

Serve the mushy peas hot.

TARTARE SAUCE

A piquant combination of creamy mayonnaise, capers, gherkins and chopped herbs.

150ml/¼ pint good-quality mayonnaise
1 heaped tablespoon capers,
    finely chopped
3 baby gherkins, finely chopped
1 tablespoon finely chopped tarragon

1 tablespoon finely chopped
    curly parsley
A good squeeze of lemon
Salt and freshly ground black pepper
    to taste

Whisk the mayonnaise until smooth, then stir in the remaining ingredients.
    Chill in the fridge until ready to serve.

POACHED SALMON WITH SAMPHIRE
AND ENGLISH BUTTER SAUCE

Light and delicately flavoured poached salmon dipped into buttery sauce is the antithesis of fish and chips. Vibrant green, long and thin samphire stems, grown along the coastal shorelines, are full of goodness and the salty taste of the sea.

Choose wild salmon fillets whenever possible and prepare the butter sauce and samphire first to prevent the fish overcooking.

THE POACHED SALMON

Perfect poached fish only requires a short cooking time in barely simmering water.

SERVES 4
150ml/¼ pint dry white wine
425ml/¾ pint water
2 shallots thinly sliced
3 slices lemon
2 bay leaves

A couple of sprigs curly parsley
6 peppercorns
Salt
4 x 200g/7oz salmon fillets

Place the wine, water, shallots, lemon, herbs and peppercorns in a shallow pan (with a fitted lid) large enough to comfortably fit the salmon fillets.

Bring the pan to a slow simmer for 5 minutes, then lay the fish fillets skin side down in the pan, cover and very gently cook for 6–8 minutes (depending on the thickness of the fish). The salmon is ready when its flakes come easily apart.

Remove from the heat and serve immediately with hot butter sauce and samphire.

ENGLISH BUTTER SAUCE

This buttery sauce is wonderful with any fish and works equally well with asparagus.

SERVES 4

20g/¾ oz plain flour
225ml/8floz equal mix of cold water
   and full-fat milk
125g/4½oz cold butter, cut into cubes

1 teaspoon lemon juice
Grated nutmeg, salt and
   ground white pepper to taste

Whisk the flour and water together in a pan until well combined, place over a medium heat and gently warm together, stirring constantly until the sauce thickens enough to coat the back of a spoon.

Pour the mixture into a heatproof bowl over slowly simmering water and gradually whisk in the butter a few bits at a time – take care, if the water boils too rapidly the sauce will spoil!

Remove the bowl from the heat and whisk in the lemon juice and seasoning to taste. Stir the sauce every once in a while to prevent a skin forming and gently re-warm just before serving.

THE SAMPHIRE

Samphire has quite an intense salty flavour, a small handful per person is plenty. Wash thoroughly, trim away the woody ends and steam for 3–4 minutes. Add a generous knob of butter to the hot samphire before serving.

THE QUEEN OF PUDDINGS

'Ah, what an excellent thing is an English pudding!' This judgment, made by a seventeenth-century French visitor, still holds true today. The English love their puddings and have perfected the fine art of pudding-making: providing warming spongy ones for a winter's day, light and fruity ones for summer, autumnal flaky pastry pies and creamy soothing nursery puddings for when you're feeling under the weather.

England's most popular puds – steamed puddings, milk puddings, sweet pies, fruit crumbles, trifles and tarts – come served with a large spoonful of nostalgia and lingering memories of cherished childhood treats. Many recipes have remained in essence unchanged for centuries. We still have a predilection for dried fruit and spices, thick cream and jam, golden syrup and custard. And many of our most treasured puds are the lucky consequence of creative cooks making the most of scraps and leftovers. But over time the welcome addition of 'exotic' ingredients such as sugar and vanilla, provisions that are now considered basic store cupboard staples, and naughty but nice influences from overseas, have combined with home-grown culinary traditions.

CUSTARD

A proper English pudding begins and ends with creamy home-made custard.

SERVES 6
560ml/1pint whole milk
1 vanilla pod, slit lengthwise
3 medium free-range egg yolks
2 medium free-range eggs
3 tablespoons golden caster sugar

Pour the milk into a saucepan and stir in the seeds scraped from the inside of the vanilla pod with the tip of a sharp knife. Gently warm together over a medium heat until bubbles start to form around the edge of the pan. Remove the pan from the heat and set to one side.

Whisk the egg yolks and whole eggs with the caster sugar in a bowl until the mixture is light and fluffy. Gradually whisk in the warm vanilla milk.

Return the custard to the pan and continue to cook over a low heat, stirring constantly, until it is thick enough to coat the back of a wooden spoon (take care not to overheat the eggs or you run the risk of lumpy custard). Serve immediately.

JAM ROLY-POLY

A real winter warmer, this steamed suet pastry jam roll is one of England's oldest puddings. Baking in the oven is a much easier option.

225g/8oz self-raising flour
110g/4oz suet
2 tablespoons caster sugar
8–9 tablespoons whole milk
7 tablespoons blackberry, raspberry or strawberry jam
Milk to seal the edges of the pudding
Soft butter to grease the greaseproof paper

Preheat the oven to 190°C/375F/Gas mark 5.

Combine the flour, suet and caster sugar in a bowl. Gradually add the milk and gently knead together until dough forms. Turn the dough out on to a lightly floured surface and roll into a roughly 23cm/9 inch x 30cm/12 inch oblong shape.

Warm the jam and spread on top, leaving 1cm/½ inch around the edge of the pastry jam-free. Brush the jam-free edges with milk and loosely roll the pastry, starting with the short edge, into a Swiss roll shape. Press along the seam and the ends of the pudding to ensure it is completely sealed.

Cut a piece of greaseproof paper into a generous oblong shape large enough to wrap the roly-poly with a pleat down the middle. Lightly butter the paper and carefully place the roly-poly in the middle, seam side down. Loosely wrap the pudding in the paper, making a pleat down the middle. Finally fold the loose ends and tuck them under the pudding.

Place the roly-poly on a baking sheet and bake in the preheated oven for 45–50 minutes. The pudding should be puffed up and look brown through the paper.

Carefully open the greaseproof paper and cut into thick slices.

FRUITY CRUMBLES – CLASSIC TO CONTEMPORARY

The humble crumble has reached the heady heights of national treasure over the course of a relatively short history – the first recipe appeared in print in the 1950s. The crumbly yet crisp topping is far less temperamental to make than pastry, which makes it a top choice for even the least experienced cook. Serve with home-made custard or buttery clotted cream.

Crumble is infinitely versatile. It can be made with almost any fruit. Below are a few basic rules worth considering before you get creative.

The weight of the fruit listed in the recipe is the prepared quantity, after stones, peel, etc. have been removed.

Soft fruits such as blackberries and blackcurrants do not need cooking first, simply cover with the crumble and pop into the preheated oven.

All fruits differ in sweetness, add sugar to suit your own personal taste.

FRUITY COMBINATIONS

Apples and blackberries are a classic combination. Soften 450g/1lb prepared Bramley apples with a splash of water and a teaspoon of vanilla extract, then combine with 275g/10oz uncooked blackberries.

Apples are also particularly good cooked with ½ teaspoon of cinnamon and a generous handful of raisins.

Cook prepared rhubarb with a heaped tablespoon of grated ginger root; water is not necessary – rhubarb contains plenty of water – but extra sugar is essential, as rhubarb is quite tart.

Try adding a handful of halved ready-to-eat dried apricots to apples or pears.

Sweet plums are perfect just as they are and only need to be simmered very briefly in the pan before they are covered with crumble.

CRUMBLE VARIATIONS

You can play around with the crumble topping – here are a few suggestions.

Replace 75g/3oz of the plain flour with rolled oats. Add a handful of sunflower seeds and a scant teaspoon of ground cinnamon to the final mixture.

Replace 25g/1oz of the plain flour with ground almonds, and stir a handful of flaked almonds or chopped hazelnuts and chopped dates into the crumbs.

TRADITIONAL CRUMBLE RECIPE

SERVES 4–6
800g/1lb 12oz prepared fruit   110g/4oz butter, diced
Golden caster sugar to taste   110g/4oz golden caster sugar
225g/8oz plain flour   60g/2½oz rolled oats

Preheat the oven to 190°C/375F/Gas mark 5.

Prepare your fruit following the basic guidance given above. Put it into a buttered medium-sized pie dish and set to one side while you mix the topping.

Sift the flour into a bowl, add the butter and rub into the flour until crumbs form. Stir in the sugar, and any 'extras', until well combined.

Pile the crumble mixture on top of the fruit, place on a baking tray and bake in the preheated oven for 30 minutes or so, until golden brown and crunchy on top.

BREAD AND BUTTER PUDDING

SERVES 4–6

425ml/¾ pint whole milk
1 vanilla pod, slit lengthwise
75g/3oz soft butter, plus extra
  to grease the dish
8 thinnish slices of day-old white
  bread cut from a good-quality
  medium-sized loaf

75g/3oz sultanas
3 large free-range eggs
50g/2oz golden caster sugar
150ml/¼ pint double cream,
  plus extra to serve
2 tablespoons Demerara sugar
Freshly grated nutmeg

Place the milk and the vanilla pod in a pan and warm over a medium heat until bubbles start to appear. Remove the pan from the heat and set to one side.

Generously butter a medium-sized ovenproof dish.

Use three-quarters of the measured quantity of butter to butter the sliced bread. Cut the slices diagonally into triangles. Arrange the bread triangles butter side up in the prepared dish, overlapping them as you do so, and make sure the crusts are facing upwards. Scatter the sultanas evenly over the top.

Place the eggs and sugar in a medium-sized bowl and whisk together until the mixture is light and fluffy. Remove the vanilla pod from the warm milk and gradually whisk the milk into the egg mixture. Add the cream and whisk until well combined.

Pour the egg custard mixture evenly over the pudding and grate a generous quantity of nutmeg on top. Set the pudding to one side for 20 minutes to allow the custard to soak into the bread. After the allotted time, dot the top of the pudding with the remaining butter and sprinkle with the Demerara sugar.

Heat the oven to 180°C/350F/Gas mark 4 and put the pudding in near the top. Bake for 30–35 minutes, until it is golden brown and crisp on top. Serve immediately with an extra drizzle of double cream.

COOK'S TIP

The addition of a tablespoon or two of brandy poured over the bread and butter slices always hits the spot. Or try replacing the bread with slices of buttered fruity panettone and a sprinkling of dried mixed peel.

GINGERY TREACLE TART

A devilishly simple way to transform stale bread into a decadent dessert.

SERVES 4–6

The pastry
225g/8oz plain flour
110g/4oz butter cut into cubes,
  plus extra to grease the tin
Cold water to combine

The filling
175g/6oz crustless good-quality
  day-old white bread for crumbs
400g/14oz golden syrup
1 heaped tablespoon treacle
1 teaspoon ground ginger
Juice and zest of a large lemon

Sift the flour into a bowl and rub in the cubed butter until crumbs form. Gradually add a little cold water to make a stiff dough. Wrap the pastry in cling film and leave it to rest in the fridge for 30 minutes.

Cut the stale bread into cubes and whiz in a food processor until finely chopped.

Preheat the oven to 200°C/400F/Gas mark 6, and grease a 20cm/8inch loose-bottomed tart tin with a little butter.

Cut away a quarter of the pastry and set to one side. Roll out the remaining pastry on a lightly floured surface to roughly 3mm/⅛ inch thick. Line the prepared tin with the pastry, cutting away any excess. Prick the pastry a few times with a fork to prevent it from rising up, then place in the preheated oven and bake blind for 10 minutes. Remove the pastry shell from the oven and reduce the temperature to 170°C/325F/Gas mark 3.

To make the filling, warm the golden syrup, treacle, ground ginger, lemon juice and zest in a small pan over a low heat until the mixture becomes runny. Combine the mixture with the breadcrumbs and use it to fill the part-cooked pastry shell.

Return the tart to the oven and bake for a further 25–30 minutes.

RICE PUDDING

This soothing nursery-style milky pudding can be traced right back to the Roman era.

SERVES 4–6

1 litre/1¾ pint whole milk
50g/2oz golden caster sugar
1 vanilla pod, slit lengthwise
110g/4oz short-grain pudding rice
150ml/¼ pint double cream

A handful of sultanas (optional)
25g/1oz diced butter,
   plus extra to grease the dish
2 heaped tablespoons brown sugar
Nutmeg

Preheat the oven to 150°C/300F/Gas mark 2 and grease a medium-sized ovenproof dish. Combine the milk with the caster sugar and the seeds scraped from the vanilla pod in a saucepan and warm over a low heat until the sugar has dissolved. Stir in the rice and simmer for a couple of minutes before adding the cream and optional sultanas.

Pour the mixture into the prepared dish, dot the butter on top, sprinkle with brown sugar and a good grating of fresh nutmeg.

Place the pudding on a low shelf in the preheated oven and cook for 1 hour, before placing on the top shelf and cooking for a further ½ hour, until the skin is caramelized and golden.

COOK'S TIP

The pudding can also be cooked on the stovetop. Combine all the ingredients in a heavy-bottomed pan and simmer over a low heat, stirring regularly, for 50 minutes. Sprinkle the thickened rice pudding with brown sugar, dot with a little butter and place under a hot grill until a caramelized skin forms.

RASPBERRY AND BANANA TRIFLE

Trifle is top of the list for special occasions, a real showstopper pudding of cake soaked in sweet sherry topped with soft fruit, custard and fresh whipped cream.

It is best to leave the trifle to chill for a few hours (even overnight), before topping with the whipped cream.

SERVES 6–8

560ml/1 pint custard (see page 134)
1 x 18cm/7inch plain sponge cake
   cut into slices, or 7 trifle sponges
150ml/¼ pint sweet sherry
2 tablespoons soft brown sugar

2 tablespoons strawberry jam
2 punnets raspberries
2 bananas, sliced
300ml/½ pint double cream
25g/1oz toasted flaked almonds

Make the custard as described on page 134, adding a dessertspoon of cornflour mixed with a splash of milk to the eggs and sugar before whisking.

Combine the sherry, sugar and jam in a small pan with a couple of tablespoons of water and gently warm over a low heat until the sugar and jam have melted.

Lay the cake slices in the bottom of a medium-sized decorative glass bowl and spoon the sherry mixture evenly over the top. Arrange the fruit on top, reserving a few raspberries for decoration. Cover the fruit with the warm custard and chill in the fridge until completely cool.

Just before serving the trifle, whip the cream until floppy, cover the custard with the cream and shape with the back of a spoon into soft peaks. Decorate the top of the trifle with toasted flaked almonds and the reserved raspberries.

SPICED BAKED APPLES

Another of England's truly great puds, so simple to prepare and so scrumptious served with cool vanilla ice cream or buttery clotted cream.

MAKES 4

110g/4oz raisins
  (or mixed chopped dried fruit)
3 tablespoons brandy
4 medium Bramley apples
2 tablespoons chopped walnuts
2 tablespoons soft light brown sugar

½ teaspoon ground cinnamon
¼ teaspoon ground cloves
¼ teaspoon ground allspice
4 teaspoons butter
1 dessertspoon Demerara sugar

Combine the raisins and brandy for an hour or so, before preparing the apples.

Preheat the oven to 180°C/350F/Gas mark 4

Core the apples with an apple corer and score around the middle of each apple with a sharp knife – this prevents the skins splitting. Place the apples, standing upright, in a baking dish.

Combine the soaked raisins with the chopped walnuts, light brown sugar and spices and pack this mixture inside the holes at the centre of the apples. Top each apple with a teaspoon of butter and sprinkle with Demerara sugar.

Place in the preheated oven and bake for 55–60 minutes, until the apples are soft but not collapsing.

Serve with the juices spooned over the top and a large scoop of ice cream or clotted cream on the side.

COOK'S TIP

To make apple dumplings simply coat the apples in pastry. Roll out 450g/1lb ready-made shortcrust pastry and cut into 4 equal-sized squares. Place a stuffed apple on each square, damp the edges with a little beaten egg and fold the pastry over the apple, pressing the edges together to make a firm seal. Brush the dumpling with beaten egg and bake in the oven for 45–55 minutes.

QUEEN OF PUDDINGS

This heady mix of vanilla custard and breadcrumbs slathered with home-made jam and fluffy meringue has adorned the English table since the seventeenth century.

SERVES 4–6

75g/3oz home-made breadcrumbs
3 large eggs, separated
150g/5oz caster sugar
570ml/1 pint full-fat milk
Grated zest of a medium
    unwaxed lemon

1 vanilla pod slit lengthwise
4 generous tablespoons home-made
    raspberry or strawberry jam
Butter to grease a medium-sized
    ovenproof shallow dish
Double cream to serve

Grease the ovenproof dish and evenly spread the breadcrumbs across the bottom.

To make the custard, whisk the separated egg yolks with 25g/1oz of the caster sugar until light and frothy. Warm the milk with the lemon zest and the vanilla pod until bubbles start to form around the edge of the pan, then remove from the heat, take out the vanilla pod and whisk the warm milk into the egg mixture. Pour the custard over the breadcrumbs and leave to soak for 20 minutes.

Preheat the oven to 180°C/350F/Gas mark 4 and bake the pudding for 30 minutes.

Remove the pudding from the oven and allow to cool for 5 minutes while you warm the jam. Carefully spread the softened warm jam on top of the pudding.

Finally make the meringue topping. Whisk the separated egg whites until peaks form and fold in the remaining caster sugar until well combined.

Spoon the meringue on top of the pudding and using the back of a spoon shape the top of the meringue into random peaks.

Return the pudding to the oven and cook for a further 15 minutes, until golden.

LEMONY SYLLABUB

This pillowy soft cream, lemon and wine concoction can be traced back to Tudor England. Whipped together in minutes it makes a simple yet rather special pud.

SERVES 4–6
55ml/2fl oz white wine
The juice and grated zest of a lemon
Optional dash of brandy
50g/2oz golden caster sugar
275ml/½ pint double cream
Shortbread biscuits and redcurrants to serve

Combine the wine, lemon juice/zest and brandy with the caster sugar in a medium-sized bowl. Stir until the sugar has completely dissolved. If you want to be thorough, it is best then to leave the mixture to stand for an hour.

Pour in the double cream and whisk together until floppy creamy peaks form.

Spoon the mixture into glasses and chill in the fridge before serving with shortbread biscuits and topped with red currants.

CHRISTMAS PLUM PUDDING

Rich, sumptuous plum pudding, the most uniquely English steamed suet pudding of them all, started its celebrated life as plum porridge, served as a filling first course at feasts. Minced mutton, onion and root vegetables were thickened with breadcrumbs and flavoured with dried fruit, sugar, spices and wine. Tempted? By the eighteenth century the porridge had evolved into a plump round pudding cooked in a floured pudding cloth, much more recognizable as the pudding we know and love today, but it was the Victorians who finally popularized the plum pudding into the brandy-flamed sweet-spiced delicacy that notoriously still lights up Christmas tables all over England to this day.

With such extravagant ingredients and a very long cooking time, plum pudding is now very much restricted to Christmas. Stir-up-Sunday (the Sunday before Advent), is traditionally the day to get started – the pudding needs a month in a cool dark place to mature (and for a fuller flavour and texture can even be kept a year). As the pudding is mixed, it is customary for every family member to stir the bowl and make a wish and small silver coins or charms are added for luck.

Brandy butter, double cream and custard are the perfect companions to a good Christmas pudding.

To serve the pudding in style, douse in brandy, ignite and carry to the table in all its flaming glory.

MINCEMEAT

If Christmas pudding sounds just too complicated, you can finish the big meal with a dainty mince pie served warm with a spoonful of rum butter.

As its name suggests, mincemeat would have contained minced meat. Now, as with Christmas pudding, suet is the only suggestion of this.

This recipe yields about 1.5kg/3¼lb of mincemeat. To make the pastry, follow the pastry recipe given with treacle tart (see page 145). This will make approximately fifteen little covered pies.

225g/8oz raisins
225g/8oz sultanas
225g/8oz currants
50g/2oz chopped candied peel
450g/1lb cooking apples, grated

225g/8oz Demerara sugar
110g/4oz suet
1 teaspoon freshly grated nutmeg
1 teaspoon mixed spice

Roughly chop the raisins, sultanas and currants in a food processor and combine with the remaining ingredients in a large bowl.

Cover the bowl and leave overnight to allow the sugar to dissolve. Seal the mincemeat in sterilized jars and store in a cool, dark place for at least a month.

To make mini pies grease a tart tin and cut pastry rounds large enough to fit each indent and lids to fit on top. Fill each tart with a teaspoon of mincemeat, moisten the edges of the pastry with milk and gently press a lid on top. Cut a small hole in the centre, brush with a little milk and bake for 15 minutes in an oven preheated to 190°C/375F/Gas mark 5 until golden brown. Dust the mince pies with icing sugar as soon as they come out of the oven.

INDEX OF RECIPES

Frances Lincoln Limited
74–77 White Lion Street
London N1 9PF
www.franceslincoln.com

Great British Cooking
Copyright © Frances Lincoln Limited 2015
Text © Carolyn Caldicott 2015
Photographs © Chris Caldicott 2015

Food styling by Carolyn Caldicott
Designed by Becky Clarke

First Frances Lincoln edition 2015

A catalogue record for this book is available
from the British Library.

978-0-7112-3508-3

9 8 7 6 5 4 3 2 1